IN TIERS OF GLORY

IN TIERS OF GLORY

The Organic Development of Catholic Church Architecture Through the Ages

MICHAEL S. ROSE

MESA FOLIO EDITIONS
MMIV

"We must return for the fire of life to other centuries,
since a night intervened between our fathers' time
and ours wherein the light was not."
Ralph Adams Cram

First Edition
Published by Mesa Folio Editions
an imprint of Aquinas Publishing Ltd.

Cover artwork by Stephanie Dalton Cowen
Photo of the author by Ron Rack

Cover design by Scott Hofmann

Mesa Folio Editions
Aquinas Publishing Ltd.
P.O. Box 11260
Cincinnati OH 4211-0260
United States of America

Ordering and distribution:
www.dellachiesa.com

ISBN 0-9676371-2-0
Library of Congress Control Number: 2004111350

Printed and bound in Canada on acid free paper

TABLE OF CONTENTS

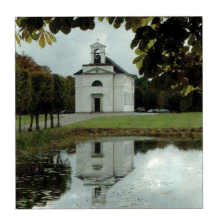

INTRODUCTION

Why history and tradition matter

ONE BASIC TENET that architects have accepted for millennia is that the built environment has the capacity to deeply affect the human person—the way he acts, the way he feels, and the way he *is*. This is possible largely because architecture has the capacity to carry meaning.

Architecture isn't inconsequential.

The Catholic Church has always understood this well. A church building is a vessel of meaning with the greatest of symbolic responsibilities: it must bear the significance of eternal truths through its material form in order to establish a sacred place destined for divine worship. The *Catechism of the Catholic Church* underlines this point when it states that "visible churches are not simply gathering places but signify and make visible the Church living in this place, the dwelling of God with men reconciled and united in Christ."[1]

This is a tall order, to be sure, and the architect today naturally wonders how a mere building can accomplish so much. Fortunately he doesn't stand alone in a vacuum, but has at his disposal more than fifteen hundred years of his craft on which to reflect.

When he turns to the Church's great architectural heritage, he discovers that from the Early Christian basilicas in Rome to the Gothic Revival churches of 20th-century America, the same canons are observed—even if they are expressed differently in each epoch—in the design of successful Catholic churches, buildings that serve both God and man as transcendental structures, transmitting eternal truths for generations to come.

Churches whose designs grow organically out of the past two millennia of churches identify themselves with the life of the Church throughout those two millennia and, by their continuity with the history and tradition of Catholic church architecture, manifest the permanence of the Catholic faith.

Santa Maria della Fiore, Italy: Built over the course of two centuries (A.D. 1296-1462) the Florence cathedral was designed by Arnolfo di Cambio. Construction progressed under the direction of several famous 'maestros,' including Giotto, Pisano, and Talenti. Although its design predated the Italian Renaissance, the dome and lantern, designed by Filipo Brunelleschi (A.D. 1420-37) is the crowning jewel of the Renaissance era.

KEY POINT

A successful church building is a work of art that acknowledges the previous greatness of the Church's architectural patrimony.

In other words, to convey that aspect of permanence rooted in historical continuity, the architectural language (the component parts and how they are put together) of churches must develop *organically* throughout time, such as when the Renaissance churches permutated into the Baroque language, or when the Gothic forms emerged from the language of the Romanesque. In both cases, the growth of the language was organic.

The 'style' may have changed, as when the semicircular arch gave way to the pointed arch. But there was no sudden break with tradition, no disregard for the churches of past centuries—arches were as much a part of the Gothic language as the Romanesque. Architects built on what they knew from the past, refining certain aspects of the language and developing others.

Architects of present and future generations need to comprehend the historical language of church architecture in order to build permanent sacred edifices for their own times and future centuries. No successful church architect can be—or even pretend to be—ignorant of the Church's historical patrimony. Continuity demands that a successful church design cannot spring from the

whims of man or the fashion of the day. A successful Catholic church building is a work of art that acknowledges the previous greatness of the Church's architectural patrimony: it refers to the past, serves the present, and informs the future.

In Tiers of Glory presents a concise history of the organic development of church architecture over the past two millennia, an organic development that has allowed the Catholic Church to be abundantly enriched with so glorious a patrimony. The approach taken in this book is consciously not a scholarly one. Rather, it is an easily understandable overview of the history of church architecture. Although *In Tiers of Glory* should serve as a welcome introduction to more substantial treatments of the many subjects addressed herein, it doesn't intend to consider the nuances and theories of the many venerable architecture historians of ages past and present. Scholarly works on church architecture certainly do serve their purposes, but *In Tiers of Glory* has the layman and architect, not the scholar and the historian, in mind.

This volume will also be useful in evaluating the unfortunate impoverishment of much of our modern church architecture, and will be helpful in proposing a new direction in church building for the 21st century, one that encourages a renewed sense of the sacred and an appreciation for history and tradition—not for an architectural renaissance for its own sake, but in order to serve future generations.

KEY POINT

Architects of our day and age need not and should not build on the unfortunate impoverishment of modern church architecture.

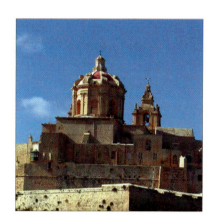

TERRA SANCTA
Old Testament Precedents

THE HISTORY AND DEVELOPMENT of Catholic church architecture can be best understood by examining the precedents consulted in every era, that is, those buildings which came *before*. We're interested first in what those precedents were, and second, how those precedents were used, how they were interpreted, and how they informed the architect's new piece of work. Any history has to start somewhere. For the church building, that beginning dates back to the very foundations of Christendom.

Although the architects of the earliest Christian churches had no 'church' buildings to look back on as informative precedents, they did look to the past to inform their designs. Their precedents? The Tabernacle in the Wilderness and Solomon's Temple, for example, as well as the form of the Roman basilica, the 'house

---

At left: King Solomon's Temple, otherwise known as the first Temple of Jerusalem.

of the King.'

The moveable tent-like sanctuary of the Hebrews, used before the erection of Solomon's Temple, is the earliest known structure in Judeo culture to establish a sacred place (*terra sancta*), one that was specifically meant to be a house of God. In Latin this tent sanctuary is called *tabernaculum,* meaning 'tent,' from which our contemporary word 'tabernacle' is derived. Whereas the tabernacles of the Christian churches are designed to hold the presence of God in His earthly Sacrament—Christ present under the appearance of bread—the Hebrew's Tabernacle in the Wilderness housed the presence of God in a different way.

Under the direction of Moses, the Tabernacle in the Wilderness was constructed to house the Ark of the Covenant. According to the Book of Exodus, God personally dictated to Moses the exact specifications. He was told to build the Ark of acacia wood in order

Mobile home: Under the direction of Moses, the Tabernacle in the Wilderness was constructed to house the Ark of the Covenant, shown above being transported by the wandering Israelites.

to accommodate the stone tablets of the Mosaic Law (Ex 25:10). This represented for the Hebrews the presence of God among them, and was their most sacred religious object and symbol. The Ark's purpose was to give the Hebrews a center for worship, a place for sacrifices and ceremonies to honor Yahweh. The Hebrews, having been released from the bonds of slavery under the Egyptians, were a nomadic tribe for forty long years as they traversed the desert in search of the Promised Land. Thus the Ark and the Tabernacle in which it was housed were designed to be easily transported.

Mobile Home

The dimensions of the Ark, as specified in Exodus 25, were approximately four feet long by three feet wide by three feet high ("two and a half cubits long, one and a half cubits wide, and one and a half cubits high"). It was covered with gold, the most precious of materials, and carried by gold-covered poles passed through rings at each corner of the Ark. On top was the golden propitiatory, decorated with cherubim on either side facing each other and spreading their wings over the propitiatory, which was also called the Seat of Mercy. It was here, between the cherubim where God was enthroned. It is because of this design spelled out in Exodus thousands of years ago that many Catholic churches have (or at least *once* had) statues of cherubim flanking the altar of sacrifice, each angel facing the tabernacle.

God also instructed Moses that a table of acacia wood covered in gold was to be built to hold the bread of sacrifice, or shewbread, which was placed before the Ark together with a golden seven-branched candlestick and the altar of incense. The Ark is rich in symbolism, and was interpreted in later centuries as one of the many symbols of Christ. The Seat of Mercy is a symbol of Christ as judge; the Mosaic tablets of the Law are a symbol of Christ as lawgiver and source of justice; and the offerings made before the Ark foreshadow the Holy Eucharist. The Church also recognizes the Ark of the Covenant as a powerful symbol of the Blessed Virgin Mary since she bore Christ within her womb, just as the Ark contained the Covenant.

KEY POINT
Architects of the early Christian centuries looked to the Tabernacle in the Wilderness and Solomon's Temple to inform their designs.

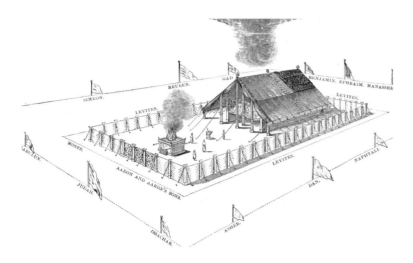

Tabernacle in the Wilderness: The 'Court of the Tabernacle' was a rectangular space screened off by curtains of fine, twisted linen. East of the entrance was the altar of sacrifice, the bronze laver, and then the tabernacle itself.

In addition to instructing Moses, God endowed Bezalel and Oholiab with the skill, knowledge, and understanding of every craft. They became masters of embroidery and in fashioning things of wood, bronze, silver, and gold. Consequently, Moses called them forth to build the tabernacle with all its furnishings, including the Ark of the Covenant. Oholiab was also endowed with the ability to teach others his crafts, and so he trained them to help with the work of building, furnishing, and decorating the portable sanctuary, which included the tent and sacred enclosure in which the tent stood. The 'court of the tabernacle' was a rectangular space screened off by curtains of fine twisted linen. These curtains were suspended from sixty pillars that each stood on bases of brass. Such a structure serves as the earliest Judeo precedent for the hierarchic separation of the sacred and the profane.

East of the entrance was the altar of sacrifice, the bronze laver (a large basin for the washing of the priests' hands), and then the tabernacle itself, the dwelling tent of God. The tabernacle was divided into two sections. To the west was the 'Holy Place.' It contained the altar of incense, the golden candlestick, and the table of shewbreads. The section to the east was called the 'Holy of Holies,' and contained the Ark of the Covenant with the propitiatory and the cherubim.

The construction was dedicated on the first day of the second year after the Hebrew's flight from Egypt. After that, the tabernacle, under the care of the Levite priests, accompanied the Hebrews through their wanderings in the desert wilderness. The Book of

KEY POINT

The design for the Tabernacle in the Wilderness provides the earliest precedent for the hierarchic separation of the sacred and the profane.

Exodus describes the Ark as sheltered in a tent that Moses pitched at some distance away from the camp. "As Moses entered the tent, the column of cloud would come down and stand at its entrance while the Lord spoke with Moses." Then, after the Hebrews crossed the Jordan into the Promised Land, the Ark remained at Galaga until it was removed to Shilo (Jos 33:1).¹

Years later King David brought the Ark up to Jerusalem, where it was once again placed in a tent until the Temple was erected as a permanent home for the Ark. Yet even before Solomon's permanent structure was built, the way in which the Ark was housed in the moveable sanctuary provides numerous precedents (e.g., the eastern orientation, the use of cherubim, the veil of the tabernacle, the

KEY POINT

Solomon reproduced in solid materials and double proportions the transient Tabernacle and its enclosure, which Moses had built in the desert.

Walled city of Jerusalem, model

Salomonic columns, St. John Lateran Basilica, Rome: These ornate, spirally twisting columns were the type used in Solomon's Temple.

priests' *laver*, the use of colonnades, and the very understanding of the Tabernacle established as a holy place and house of God set apart from the profane) that informed the architects of the Christian era in establishing holy places that were houses of God.

Domus Dei

King Solomon's Temple, otherwise known as the first Temple of Jerusalem, provides the second great precedent for the church architect. Solomon reproduced in solid materials and double proportions the transient Tabernacle and its enclosure, which Moses had built in the desert: "Thou hast given command to build a temple on thy holy mountain, and an altar in the city of thy habitation, a copy of the holy tent which thou didst prepare from the beginning" (Wis 9:8), the entire plan of which is therefore outlined. The Temple, completed in seven-and-a-half years in 966 B.C., was built in great splendor and dedicated with much magnificence—"I have built thee an exalted house, a place for thee to dwell in for ever," Solomon proclaims—as described in 1 Kings 8, and elaborated upon by the prophet Ezekiel in 2 Chron 3-4,[2] who describes in depth the construction and design of the Temple.

Solomon employed King Hiram of Tyre to sail the Mediterranean in order to obtain for him the finest materials (e.g., the timbers of Lebanese cypresses), skilled craftsmen, and renowned Phoenician smiths to build the great edifice, which the Hebrews called *Bet*

KEY POINT
Solomon's Temple stood on the highest point of Mount Moriah, on the spot where Abraham made ready to sacrifice his son Isaac.

[2] King Solomon's Temple is repeatedly referred to as both "the house of God" and "house of the Lord" throughout 2 Chronicles 3-4. Furthermore, in 1 Kings 9:1-3, God Himself confirms that the Temple is truly a house of God: "When Solomon had finished building the house of the Lord and the king's house and all that Solomon desired to build, the Lord appeared to Solomon a second time, as he appeared to him at Gibeon. And the Lord said to him, 'I have heard your prayer and supplication, which you have made before me; I have consecrated this house which you have built, and put my name there forever.'"

'City on a hill,' **Midina, Malta:** The concept of the church as a 'city on a hill' hearkens back to the time of Solomon, when the king built his temple on the highest point of Mount Moriah.

KEY POINT
Well before the Incarnation of Christ, the great Jewish masters provided the Christian architects and craftsmen of later centuries fundamental principles to guide them in establishing "houses of God" for their own era.

Yehovah (House of Yahweh). According to 2 Chronicles the Temple stood on the highest point of Mount Moriah, on the spot where Abraham made ready to sacrifice his son Isaac, and where, centuries later, King David erected an altar of holocausts to the Lord.[3] Such conspicuous siting serves as the earliest precedent for understanding our churches as 'city on a hill.'

One of the most interesting and perhaps peculiar elements of the Temple design were the ornate, spirally twisting columns known today as salomónicas. The same columns were used in the design of both Constantine's Old St. Peter's (324-329) and the present St. Peter's Basilica in Rome. Gianlorenzo Bernini (1598-1680), the great Baroque master, used King Solomon's column design to support the baldacchino over the papal altar in the 'new' St. Peter's, but the Salomónic order was most commonly used in the Baroque altars and reredoses of Spain and Portugal and their dominions. Thus, even well before the Incarnation of Christ, the great Jewish masters, under instructions from God and under the direction of Moses and King Solomon, provided the Christian architects and craftsmen of later centuries fundamental principles to guide them in establishing houses of God for their own era and for eternity. It is highly significant that God Himself confirms both the title 'house of God' (or 'house of the Lord') and the eternal nature of the great edifice of Solomon when the Lord said to him, "I have heard your prayer and supplication, which you have made before me; I have consecrated this house which you have built, and put my name there forever" (1 Kings 9:3).[4]

[3] "Then Solomon began to build the house of the Lord in Jerusalem on Mount Moriah, where the Lord appeared to David his father, at the place that David had appointed, on the threshing floor of Ornan the Jebusite" (2 Chron 3:1).

[4] When Nebuchadnezzar captured Jerusalem in 598 B.C., the Ark and the rest of the treasures of Solomon's Temple were taken to Babylon as spoil. From that time on the whereabouts of the Ark have been unknown.

HOUSE OF CHRIST THE KING
Churches of the Early Christian Centuries

THE EARLIEST CHRISTIAN 'houses of God' not only established themselves as permanent sacred places, they reflected in many ways the divinely inspired design and construction of Solomon's Temple and its transient precursor, the Tabernacle in the Wilderness. But because of the religious persecutions of Christians, the faithful were not able to build such great edifices to the glory of God until three hundred years after Christ's death on the Cross.

Constantine the Great, a solar henotheist (a pagan sun-worshipper), was the first Roman emperor to favor Christianity. Consequently, he became the first great patron of Christian architecture. The Edict of Milan, issued by Constantine and his co-emperor Licinius in A.D. 313, mandated toleration of the Christian religion. Public worship of Christ was not only no longer forbidden, but Constantine, because of divine inspiration, favored Christianity over the pagan cults and made large financial donations to the Church. Thus Constantine was very influential in the development of Christian architecture.

Transforming Caligula's Circus

In Rome, Constantine commissioned the church now known as Old St. Peter's. The site upon which this earliest of Roman churches was built has a notorious history. It began as the garden of Agrippina, the mother of Caligula (A.D. 12-41), a Roman emperor particularly noted for his cruelty, and the grandmother of Emperor Nero. Caligula built a 'circus' there where many appalling spectacles took place in the midst of a bloodthirsty crowd, not the least of which was the martyrdom of many Christians. St. Peter, the first pope, was crucified upside-down at that site. Thus, it was

At left: The Basilica of St. Paul Outside-the-Walls, one of the four patriarchal basilicas of Rome.

23

Temple of Antoninus and Faustina, Rome: (A.D. 141) Built to honor the Emperor and his wife, it is the only building in the Roman Forum that indicates the monumental size of Roman temples. It was saved from destruction when it was consecrated a church.

KEY POINT
The basilica ('house of the king') was the noblest form of architecture in the Roman Empire at the time of Constantine and was thought therefore to be the most appropriate to adopt for the Christian church building.

Pagan Basilica of Maxentius, Rome: (A.D. 310-313) Architectural historian Sir Banister Fletcher wrote in his *A History of Architecture* that this Roman basilica "is in many respects a prototype of a Gothic structure."

considered the ideal spot upon which the primatial church in Rome should be constructed.

Constantine's architects were inspired by the Roman basilica (the 'house of the King,' from the Greek *basileus*). Between 184 and 121 B.C. there were built in the Forum at Rome the basilicas of Porcia, Fulvia, Sempronia, and Opimia. These public buildings, designed to beautify the Forum, were used primarily for purposes of lawmaking (halls of justice) and commerce (marketplaces). The Roman basilica was the noblest form of architecture in the Empire at the time of Constantine and was thought therefore to be the most appropriate to adopt for the Christian church building.

According to the architect Vitruvius, the basic Roman basilica consisted of a roofed hall having a wide central aisle, separated from two side aisles by a colonnade on either side. The walls of the hall rose high above the aisle roofs and used clerestory windows to admit light. At one end of the great hall's central aisle, separated from the hall by a triumphal arch, was a raised platform on which stood an altar of sacrifice. The long hall terminated in a semicircular area which had seats for the Roman officials. Some basilicas had a pitched roof constructed of wooden rafters, while others were vaulted with masonry.

Adapting the Roman Basilica

The architects of Old St. Peter's adapted the general form of the Roman basilica for Christian worship. The basilica was the building type that enjoyed the greatest longevity, was constructed of the finest materials, and emphasized the vertical dimension. Furthermore, it was perfectly suitable to manifest the symbolic path to God and salvation, which in the basilica leads the Christian from the profane outside world toward the sanctuary in distinct stages. In contrast, the pagan temples, because they were designed as sanctuaries for false gods, and because they could not accommodate an assembly of hundreds—only priests were permitted to enter— were deemed inappropriate for the purposes of the Christian church.

Temple of Divus Romulus, Rome: Built in the 4th century to deify Romulus, the son of the Emperor Maxentius, it was converted in a later century to the Church of Ss. Cosmas and Damian.

KEY POINT
Pagan temples, because they were designed as sanctuaries for false gods, were deemed inappropriate for the purposes of the Christian church.

Section, Old St. Peter's Basilica, Rome: Built in the 4th century on the site of Nero's Circus, it was the first of the patriarchal basilicas.

25

Triumphal Arch of Constantine, Rome: Built in A. D. 312 in honor of the Emperor's victory over Maxentius. The triumphal arch was adapted to the Christian basilica and used to separate the nave from the sanctuary.

KEY POINT
St. John Lateran, St. Paul Outside-the-Walls, St. Mary Major, and St. Peter's are known as the four 'patriarchal basilicas' of Rome.

The architects also set a precedent by building over the tomb of a martyr, a practice that became common in early Christian Rome. Thus, the Christian basilica, as reflected in the design of Old St. Peter's, consisted of an oblong space divided into a central hall (later called the nave), with side aisles separated by a colonnade. At the eastern end of the nave was the raised platform of the sanctuary, terminated with a domed, semicircular apse. At the center of the sanctuary stood a canopied altar, and behind it the bishop's chair (cathedra), with seats for the priests and deacons on either side. The sanctuary was separated from the nave by a triumphal arch, just as in the pagan basilicas. Because the sanctuary with altar and cathedra were spiritually most important in the hierarchy of the Christian basilica, the apse and the triumphal arch were typically decorated richly with paintings or mosaics.

The altar was made of stone, and its prominence was emphasized not only by the triumphal arch and the canopy of the baldacchino, but by its placement on a stepped platform. Beneath the altar was often placed the remains of a saint, if the building was not actually built over the saint's tomb. In the case of Old St. Peter's, the body of the first pope, except for his skull, was placed in a crypt directly beneath the altar, as it is in the present structure designed by Bramante and Michelangelo.

The art and architecture of the basilica worked together in unity to lead the eye down the central aisle of the nave toward the altar at the center of the sanctuary. The triumphal arch and the apse further emphasized the importance and priority given to the altar upon which the Holy Sacrifice of the Mass was offered by the bishop and his clergy.

Although the pagan basilica form was more or less a simple rectangle in design, the architects modified the form for the Christian basilica by adding a short transept to either side of the nave near the sanctuary. Consequently they created the 'cruciform' plan. Constantine's architects made one other conspicuous addition: the atrium, a large open forecourt cut off from the outside world by high walls and surrounded by cloisters with sloping roofs. A gateway resembling a triumphal arch gave access from the street, and the open-air interior was made up of gardens, usually with a large fountain at its center.

Some of the other significant Roman basilicas of the early Church were St. John Lateran (324), St. Paul Outside-the-Walls (386), and St. Mary Major (432). Along with St. Peter's, these churches became known as the 'patriarchal basilicas of Rome.' The two most unaltered basilicas from the Early Christian era, however, are Santa Sabina (422) in Rome and Sant'Apollinare (520) in Ravenna. All of these churches reflect the typical basilica arrangement used in every century since the reign of Constantine.

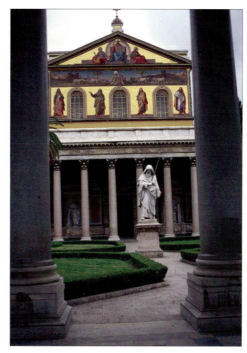

St. Paul Outside-the-Walls, Rome: one of the four 'patriarchal basilicas of Rome,' St. Paul's was built in the 4th century, but was destroyed in 1823. It was subsequently rebuilt on the original design.

KEY POINT
Works of sacred art, just as the basilicas themselves, became 'vessels of meaning,' transmitting religious truths by the use of both image and symbol.

Santa Sabina Church, Rome: (A. D. 425) Its basilican plan has nave and aisles separated by 24 Corinthian columns. Its baldacchino dates from the 11th century and its mosaics from the 8th.

Basilica of St. Mary Major, Rome: Built in the 5th century, it is the only church for which there is evidence that it was originally a Pagan basilica.

Vessels of Meaning

Aside from the major contribution of the basilican form, the early Christian Church, beginning in the 4th century, developed the use of the image in religious art that came to decorate the interiors of early church structures.

Because 4th-century Christianity was still seen principally as the religion of the poor to whom abstract symbolism meant little, visual images began to appear in Christian artwork of the new basilica-style churches. Madonna and Child, the Annunciation, the Nativity, and other New Testament subjects began to appear in Christian painting.

These early churches were first decorated with frescoes, and later more commonly with mosaics. These sacred images, however, were not valued for their own sake as decoration or objects of worship (as in pagan art), but for the spiritual significance of their content. These images, just as the basilicas themselves, became 'vessels of meaning,' transmitting religious truths by the use of both image and symbol.

In the late 6th century Pope St. Gregory the Great authoritatively ratified the use of religious imagery in churches. Many were concerned that this practice might be idolatrous, as it was regarded as such by the Hebrews in light of the Second Commandment, and as it was practiced by the pagan cults of pre-Christian Rome.

St. Gregory clarified that sacred paintings and mosaics were "books of the poor and illiterate, a means of imparting a knowledge of Scripture." He also recognized their capacity to raise man's thoughts from the temporal to the eternal. His emphasis, however, was placed on assuring Christians that these images were not for the purposes of worshipping.

The contributions of Christian architects and artists of the early Christian era are hardly insignificant. Both the basilica form and religious imagery have been used in countless churches of every century since. The basic basilica form was used as the prototype for churches of western Christendom in the Romanesque, Gothic, Renaissance, Baroque, and Revivalist epochs that followed upon the early Christian era.

Temple of Saturn, Rome: (A.D. 284)

Fresco of St. Peter: Inside church at Agia Triada archeological site, Crete, Greece.

KEY POINT
Aside from the major contribution of the basilican form, the early Christian Church, beginning in the 4th century, developed the use of imagery in religious art.

29

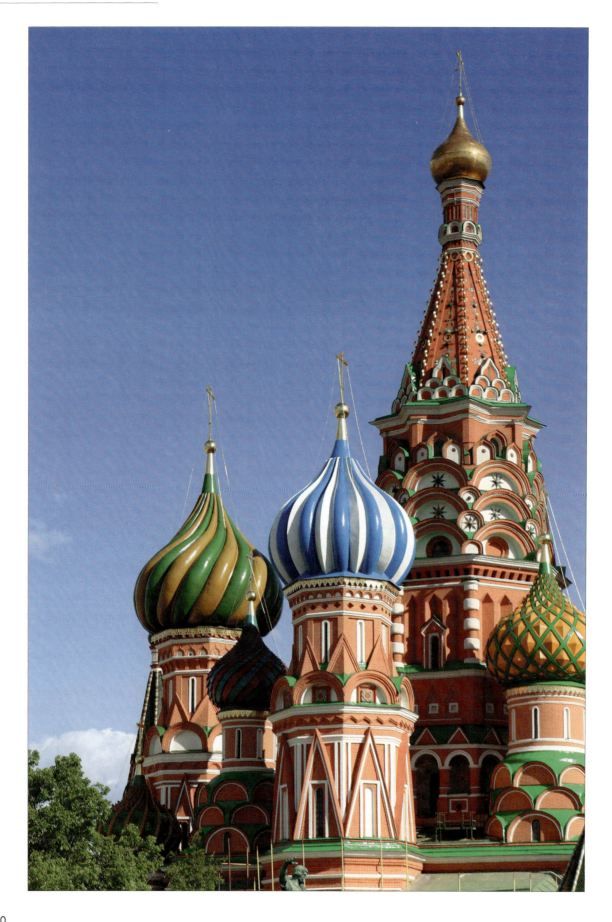

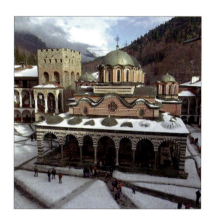

OUT OF THE EAST
The Architecture of Byzantium

CONSTANTINE'S NEW CAPITAL, built on the remains of the ancient Greek city-state called Byzantium, is important to understanding Byzantine architecture. In 323, the Emperor of the West ruled over both the Eastern and Western empires. Only a few years later did Constantine transfer the imperial capital from Rome to the new city of Constantinople, which became the center of Byzantine art and culture.

To preserve unity in the empire, churches that were commissioned during Constantine's reign reflected the plans of the Roman basilica used in the Western churches. Following the political schism of the Roman Empire in about 395, an ever-widening breach between the cultures of the East and West produced a distinctively Byzantine art and architecture. This is readily verified by the church architecture of the 5th

At left: the 'cheerful decoration' of St. Basil's Cathedral in Moscow includes nine bulb-like domes.

and 6th centuries. During the reign of Emperor Justinian the Great (527-65), Byzantine churches broke away from using the Roman basilica style in favor of a hybrid between the centralized domed plans of the martyrium (a shrine for a martyr) and the longitudinal plan of the basilica.

The architecture of Hagia Sophia (the Church of Divine Wisdom), completed by Justinian in 537, set the precedent for the Byzantine 'domed basilica,' while the Church of the Holy Apostles, also in Constantinople, set the precedent for the 'domed church.' These two models became the subject of many variations based on the Greek cruciform plan.

Until the Eastern Empire fell into the hands of the Turks in 1453, Byzantine architects generally designed centrally planned domed churches, with entrance and apse facing one another on the horizontal axis. It is important to note, however, that the altar of the

Hagia Sophia, Constantinople: (A.D. 532-537) Built by the Emperor Justinian on the site of two previous basilican churches, it represents the quintessential Byzantine church. Ironically it later became the most important mosque in Constantinople.

KEY POINT

After the Great Schism of 1054, which severed the Eastern Church from Rome, Byzantine church architecture came to be universally identified with the Orthodox Church.

Byzantine church was always placed at the east end of the church in the apse, never at the center of the church beneath the dome.

The dome was considered an essential part of the Byzantine church, and regarded as symbolic of heaven and as an actual part of the New Jerusalem—distant and untouchable yet visible and inspiring. Often times a mosaic image of Christ, the natural focus of the Byzantine world of sacred images, would decorate the central dome as well as the apse of the sanctuary, the two most prominent positions in the church.

Noteworthy, too, is that Christ was not usually depicted by the Byzantines as the Son of God or the Good Shepherd as he was in the West, but rather as Pantocrator—meaning Ruler of all Creation or Judge of the Apocalypse.

Hagia Sophia, Constantinople: (A.D. 532-537)

St. John of Rila Monastery, Bulgaria: Founded in the 10th century, the monastery was rebuilt in the 13th century. In the 15th century, when Bulgaria fell to the Ottoman Turks, the monastery was abandoned for a short time, but in the second half of the same century it was restored. In later centuries the monastery was plundered several times.

A Crack in the Foundation

After the Great Schism of 1054, which severed the Eastern Church from Rome, Byzantine church architecture came to be universally identified with the Orthodox Church, while in the West the churches of the Latin rite typically maintained variations of the cruciform basilica plan. The Byzantine style eventually extended throughout the Orthodox world, taking on various specific national 'looks,' especially in Greece, Armenia, Georgia, Russia,[1] and the north Balkans.

The architecture of Byzantium also highly influenced some notable churches of the West. The Cathedral of San Marco in Venice (1063-94, see p. 37), considered by many art historians to be the most beautiful of all churches of the Byzantine style, provides a prime example. Venice had close trading ties with the East, and Venetian architecture at the beginning of the second millennium reflected this close association. Because San Marco is an edifice built on such a monumental scale, the architects did not adopt the simple domed cruciform plan, but used a variation. Designed with a central dome over a Greek-cross floor plan with four smaller domes constructed over each arm of the cross, it reflected the look of Constantinople's Church of the Holy Apostles, yet on a grander scale.

San Marco's famous gold mosaics are perhaps more revealing of the Byzantine influence than even the form or arrangement of the building. Most of the mosaicists who worked at the Venetian

[1] The church architecture of Old Russia is best exemplified by Moscow's St. Basil (see p. 30). Built 100 years after the fall of Constantinople, the church was commissioned by Ivan the Terrible as an act of thanksgiving for the conquest of Kazan. The use of 'cheerful decoration' and the nine bulb-like domes that cap the church reveals the Oriental influence. Each dome is conspicuously decorated, whether scalloped, twisted, fluted, or reticulated, and each is colored uniquely. The style is immediately recognizable as 'Russian Byzantine.'

Church at Pecs, Hungary: Originally built as a mosque during the Turkish occupation, it was later transformed into a Catholic church.

Palatine Chapel, Palermo, Sicily: (A.D. 1132) The chapel of the Royal Palace, pictured here, is famous for its elaborate colored mosaics.

cathedral originally came from Byzantium. They were masters of their craft who had immigrated to Italy to find work after Iconoclasm had destroyed their livelihood in the East. The heresy of Iconoclasm caused the destruction of images used for religious purposes. Beginning in the 8th century, many of the Eastern clergy (who considered themselves enlightened in the Gnostic sense) were opposed to the use of images, not only because they associated imagery with the pagan cults of antiquity, but also because they misinterpreted St. John when he taught that God should be worshipped "in spirit and truth" (Jn. 4:23).

The common lay people, however, overwhelmingly supported the use of imagery in their churches, as they felt a need to be guided and inspired in their worship by pictorial art. Nevertheless, Emperor Leo III (680-741) prohibited religious images in all churches

Monastery of S. Luke of Stiris, Greece: 11th century

Rotunda Church of St. George, Sofia, Bulgaria: Three layers of frescoes were recently discovered in this church, the earliest dating back to the 10th century.

of the Eastern Empire, which ended in his excommunication by Pope St. Gregory II in 731. Despite the pope's intervention, the iconoclastic doctrine was rigorously enforced. Iconophiles were brutally persecuted. Monks who favored the use of icons were sometimes blinded or exiled.

The following century saw the destruction of nearly all existing religious images throughout Byzantium, and new mosaics were not commissioned. In 787, the Church formally condemned Iconoclasm at the Second Council of Nicea, decreeing that painting and mosaic images representing the divine were permissible and worthy of veneration. Even so, a second wave of Iconoclasm took hold during the 9th century and religious images portrayed in Byzantine art were either forbidden or frowned upon for several centuries thereafter. The use of three-dimensional sculptures depicting Christ and the saints was never accepted in the East. Sculpture remained a forbidden art and has never been incorporated into Byzantine church architecture.

But even with those imposed limits on Byzantine art, the contributions of Byzantium were unique and important to the development of church architecture for many centuries to come.

KEY POINT

In 787, the Church formally condemned Iconoclasm, decreeing that painting and mosaic images representing the divine were permissible and worthy of veneration.

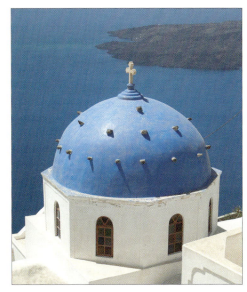

Byzantine-inspired Greek dome, Santorini: The Byzantine forms extended throughout the Orthodox world, including throughout the Greek islands.

Cathedral of San Marco, Venice: (A.D. 1063-1094) considered by many art historians to be the most beautiful of all churches of the Byzantine style. The original Church of San Marco was destroyed by fire in 976. After the fire, Venetians searched the rubble for the remains of St. Mark's body, which were brought to the church from Alexandria in 828. The remains could be found nowhere. When construction of the present basilica was starting, a solemn fast was called, and prayers were offered in the hope that the lost relics would be found. On June 25, 1063, as a procession moved through the new basilica, a bright light suddenly shone from a pillar near the altar of St. James. Part of the wall of masonry fell away, and a sweet fragrance filled the church. It was here that the body of St. Mark was rediscovered. It had been bricked into the wall by a careless workman.

Opposite page: Upenski Cathedral, Finland, the seat of Helsinki's Russian Orthodox Church, it has thirteen 'onion domes,' representing Christ and His apostles.

37

THE FIRST GREAT RENAISSANCE
Carolingian and Romanesque Church Architecture

AFTER THE FALL OF ROME in the 5th century, the architecture of the West developed independently of Byzantium, with few exceptions in places like Venice and Sicily. During the years that the invading Germanic tribes ruled in place of the Romans—from the 5th century until the 9th—there was little development in church architecture. The various barbarians were slowly Romanized and eventually accepted Christianity.

During these years known to some as the Dark Ages, little creativity was manifested in barbarian culture. Consequently, the churches constructed during these times merely reflected the Roman forms of the early Christians.

In Spain, for example, the churches, although imitating the plan of the basilica, were small and primitive compared to the huge church edifices

At left: Mont St. Michel, crowned by the Benedictine Abbey of Saint-Michel.

commissioned by Constantine. The barbarians simply tried to approximate what the Romans had done. Common were timber-roofed basilicas with a three-bay nave and aisles, separated by an arcade of round arches set on square piers.

Despite their relatively small size, these modest churches were built as permanent structures (using stones as the primary building blocks) and used artistic means in order to render an iconography that would both educate and lift man's soul to God. The artwork, however, was admittedly much cruder than that of early Christian Rome.

The architecture built by the invading tribes is sometimes known as 'barbarian' but more commonly as 'pre-Romanesque.' Although such architecture formed a bridge between the Roman Empire and medieval Europe, it is of little significance in the scheme of Western church architecture.

Pisa Cathedral, Italy: (A. D. 1063-92) resembles early Christian basilicas in plan with its long rows of columns connected by arches.

Santa Fosca Church, Torcello, Italy: (A. D. 1108) This small church on Torcello island in the Venetian lagoons (where East meets West) provides an excellent example of a mixture of the Byzantine and Romanesque influences.

Carolingian Restoration of the West

When Charlemagne, King of the Franks, was crowned Emperor of Rome by the pope at the beginning of the 9th century, he regarded the restoration of the West as both a spiritual and a political duty. He set about to revive the traditions of ancient Rome in light of the universal call to recognize Christ as the center of the new emerging culture. To Carolingian men, ancient Rome meant Rome of the Christian era, and it was this aspect alone that they sought to revive in their art and architecture that was built predominately in the lands of France and Germany.

This was the beginning of the first great Renaissance in Christendom. It found expression in architecture based on the Italian prototype and the high artistic expressions of late antiquity. At the same time, however, some aspects of Carolingian architecture were decidedly innovative in spirit.

The Emperor's architects and builders not only looked to the past but they were unconsciously laying the foundation for a distinctive Western architecture of the future. All this is owed directly to Charlemagne, who ordered that the new architecture reflect antiquity, that churches be built of stone (the most durable of materials available), and that the basilican scheme be used as the standard arrangement for churches. Charlemagne's builders returned to using the antique Roman method of masonry

Pisa Cathedral, Italy: along with the baptistery, the campanile (the famous 'leaning tower of Pisa'), and the Santo Campo, it forms one of the most well known architectural attractions in the Western world.

construction—ashlar—rather than the more primitive methods of rubble walling used by the barbarian tribes.

The basilican scheme adopted from the Romans of antiquity was modified somewhat during this era. While still maintaining both the axial arrangement and the Latin cross plan created by the use of side transepts, the Carolingian basilicas often added additional apses flanking the larger, main apse in order to accommodate side altars when the bishop wished to dedicate a church to more than one saint.

A more important innovation of Carolingian churches was the addition of the 'westwerk,' a tall structure flanked by two towers containing staircases placed at the west end of the building at the

KEY POINT
A 19th-century French archeologist coined the term 'Romanesque' to describe the art and architecture that adapted the forms from the ancient Roman empire.

Chiesa di Montalto, Messina, Sicily: The dome from Santuario di Cristo Re can be seen in the background.

Mainz Cathedral, Germany: (A. D. 1036) Along with the cathedral at Worms, this is representative of German expression of Romanesque.

KEY POINT
Although brick, marble, and terra cotta were common materials used to construct the new churches, the most important material was stone, continuing the Roman tradition of sturdiness.

nave's entrance. A low entrance hall, precursor to the narthex (or vestibule) of later centuries, supported a large loft above it that opened directly onto the nave. The stair towers on both sides accessed the loft. This is perhaps the most distinctive aspect of Carolingian architecture. Yet, the Carolingian motifs were not synthesized into a coherent architectural style. That wouldn't happen until the flowering of the Romanesque period.

Ordering the Chaos

Once order finally triumphed over chaos in the Holy Roman Empire, a unified architectural style wholly emerged. Despite the lingering lack of political unity throughout Europe, the Church was

Trani Cathedral, Italy: (A. D. 1099-1197) Located in Italy's Bari province, known for its old Romanesque churches, which also included the cathedrals of Bari, Giovinazzo, Malfetta, Ruvo, Canosa, and Bittonto.

Lessay Abbey, France: (A.D. 1056) This Benedictine church is touted as the "purest" Norman Romanesque building still standing today. It was twice nearly destroyed: first during the war between France and Navarre in 1356, and during World War II in 1944.

able to effect a certain unity in the architecture of her churches. Nevertheless, the style developed in its own way in each of the European countries. For example, in the northern countries the roofs were steeply sloped to throw off the rain and snow, while the windows tended to be large in order to admit as much sunlight as possible. Small windows and thick walls with gently sloped roofs characterized Romanesque churches of the southern countries. But these regional differences were little more than superficial variations. More importantly, the Romanesque churches were all inspired by the same architectural ideals.

Many of these churches were built using the remains of the Roman buildings that had stood unused for centuries. Columns, decorations, and other pieces of these old buildings—hewn stone, carved capitals, and sculptured friezes—were used to construct the new forms. Thus, a 19th-century French archeologist coined the term 'Romanesque' to describe the art and architecture that adapted the forms from the ancient Roman empire. Following the lead of Charlemagne, the patrons of this era used classical Roman masonry construction to build permanent structures to serve as their houses of God.

Although brick, marble, and terra cotta were the most common materials used to construct the new churches, the most important material was stone, continuing the Roman tradition of sturdiness

KEY POINT
Many Romanesque churches were built using the remains of the Roman buildings that had stood unused for centuries.

San Martino Cathedral, Pietrasanta, Italy: (A.D. 1223) Located in Tuscany in an area known for its marble.

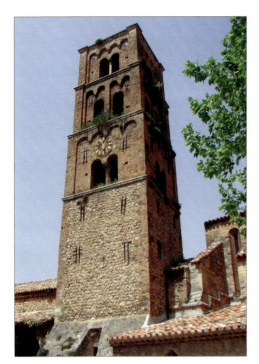

Notre Dame Church, Moustiers Ste. Marie, France: (12ᵗʰ century) topped by a four-level Lombard Romanesque bell tower, carved from golden-brown volcanic ash.

and amplitude. While the Romans of late-antiquity and the early Christians also used masonry construction, the anonymous Romanesque builders were the first to utilize stone as a sculptable, carvable material. Furthermore, craftsmen became much more accurate in their stonecutting, and their jointing became so precise that they no longer relied on mortar joints. This affected the articulation of interior walls in that the stone units, because of their inherent beauty and the skill of the craftsmen, were often used as the decoration itself instead of surface ornamentation.

The most remarkable advancement was the reintroduction of vaulting. Even by the time the early Christians raised the first basilicas, the Roman art of vaulted construction was all but lost to them. Constantine's architects roofed their churches not with vaulted ceilings but with timber trusses. Ancient Roman vaulting techniques became customary in the architecture of the late Romanesque period, and were developed further in the Gothic structures of later centuries.

Another important Romanesque development in church planning involved the intersection of the nave and the transepts, known as the 'crossing.' The Romanesque builders often extended the nave beyond the point of intersection. This enabled them to articulate the crossing by creating equally sized heavy arches on each of its four sides. This required the width of the transepts to be equal to

Abbey Church of Mont St. Michel: (A.D. 1132-44) is the crowning jewel of this fortified monastery town (also see illustration p. 38).

Ss. Peter & Paul Abbey, Romanmotier, Switzerland: Built in the 10th and 11th centuries, it is similar in style to the French Abbey at Cluny.

that of the central aisle of the nave. The result was a comprehensive internal order centered on the perfect square of the crossing. More importantly, this new engineering dictated by the strong weight-bearing structure of the four crossing arches enabled the builders to construct towers over the crossing to further emphasize this central element. Indeed, towers became very important to Romanesque churches, whether built over the crossing, at the west end of the building, or separate from the church itself.

The most well-known examples of the Romanesque are the cathedrals of Pisa and Monreale in Italy; Salamanca and Santiago de Compostela in Spain; Cluny, Vézaley, and Mont St. Michel in France; and the cathedrals of Mainz, Worms, and Speyer in Germany. Many of the monasteries and abbey churches of England, destroyed by King Henry VIII after his break with Rome, were also built in the Romanesque.

During the 11th century, the Church saw a remarkable flourishing of the monastic system that had been fostered by Charlemagne centuries earlier. During this time, monastic orders such as the Benedictines, Cistercians, and Carthusians provided the foundations of culture and learning throughout England and Europe by educating youths at their monastery schools. Monks and their pupils were often the designers of the Romanesque churches that sprang up during these centuries.

KEY POINT
One important Romanesque development in church planning involved the intersection of the nave and the transepts, known as the 'crossing.' Thus the cruciform plan was born.

St. Sernin Basilica, Toulouse, France: (A.D. 1080-96) The central octagonal tower dates from A.D. 1250 and reflects certain Gothic elements.

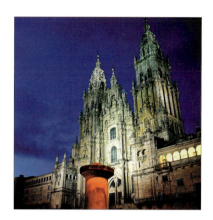

THE LONG AND WINDING ROADS
Pilgrimage Shrines and Churches

THE CHURCHES OF THE ROMANESQUE era were the fruits of an agrarian Christian culture. Not only did they serve as places of worship and devotion, but also as centers of the community.

One aspect of the agrarian Catholic culture in medieval Europe was the rise in popularity of the Christian pilgrimage. A pilgrimage usually involved a long, arduous journey to a sacred place known as a shrine. The veneration of martyrs led to the building of these shrines to which the faithful often times came in droves. This practice gave rise to the 'pilgrimage church.' The more geographically inaccessible these churches were, the more excitement they seemed to generate. The pilgrims willingly embraced the hardships endured in crossing rugged terrain.

Spiritual rewards, acts of penance, proof of

At left: Church in Rioja, Spain, built along the pilgrimage route to Santiago de Compostela

devotion, and insurance against famine and plague were some of the reasons pilgrims traveled for days to an often out-of-the-way shrine. Others journeyed to the pilgrimage churches to seek the intercession of particular saints for cures of the sick. Whatever the reason for his trip, the pilgrim enjoyed a special status as he made his way to the shrine. He could obtain a sacred shrine badge, which put the pilgrim above all laws but those of the Church. During his sacred excursion he was exempt from taxes, debts, arrest, or confiscation of his property, and was often honored or entertained, as the people believed that anyone aiding a pilgrim shared in his grace.

The effects of the pilgrims on the towns along the popular routes were many. Markets bustled, building and shipping industries boomed, churches were crowded, and customs, songs, and tables were exchanged. Souvenirs and art objects carried by the

pilgrims helped spread artistic styles from one country to another, and the necessity of accommodating large crowds led to a series of new churches along these pilgrimage routes.

A Little Help Along the Way

The typical pilgrimage of the Middle Ages usually took about a year. Written guidebooks advised the length of a day's journey, what to carry along, and how to protect oneself from personal misfortune. The pilgrims sometimes faced not only the rugged terrain of the route and the possibility of a lengthy illness, but some pilgrimage routes were infested with bandits who were waiting to assault travelers. Thus the medieval pilgrim faced daily the chance that he might be not only cheated, but attacked, robbed, and even murdered. For this reason, most pilgrims traveled in large groups. No matter what the discomforts, however, a pilgrimage was usually

KEY POINT
The veneration of martyrs led to the building of shrines to which the faithful often came in droves. This practice gave rise to the 'pilgrimage church.'

Village church in Roussillon, France: (11th century)

San Miniato Church, Florence: (A.D. 1013) This pilgrimage church is unique in that its raised eastern portion has a crypt (with a saint's tomb) that is open to the nave.

KEY POINT
The medieval pilgrim faced daily the chance that he might be not only cheated, but attacked, robbed, and even murdered. For this reason, most pilgrims traveled in large groups.

a pleasant occasion, and the pilgrim received not a little help along the way.

It was traditional advice that "if ye owe any pilgrimages, pay them hastily," and those who could muster the necessary funds rushed to don pilgrim's garb. If funds were not available, however, all was not lost. In these times the pilgrim penitent received great sympathy from his friends, who considered it their duty to aid his pilgrimage. For this purpose guilds were established. When in need, the penitent came to the guild for financial assistance. Nor was it only the guilds that aided the pilgrim, but also the Church and the state joined forces for his protection. Laws laid down in the 12th century threatened excommunication to anyone found guilty of cheating, attacking, or robbing a pilgrim. Toll fees were abolished for them, guide service was made available, and a charitable system of shelters and hospitals developed where the voyager could receive free benefits ranging from a haircut to shoe repair.

Underground Devotion

The importance placed on pilgrimages affected the care and attention given to the building of these popular churches. Many

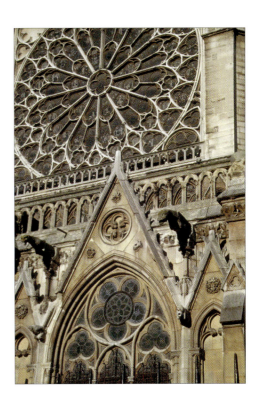

Notre Dame de la Grande, Poitiers: (11ᵗʰ century) An important pilgrimage stop on the route to Santiago de Compostela, the church is renowned for its elaborately sculpted western facade.

KEY POINT
The veneration of relics and the popularity of pilgrimages had several interesting consequences for church architecture, including the development of crypts, ambulatories, and radiating side shrines.

were erected in the Romanesque centuries and others later during the Gothic era. All were of great significance to laity and clergy alike. These pilgrimage shrines not only reminded the faithful of Christ and His ultimate sacrifice on the Holy Cross, but they also illuminated the Church's belief in the communion of saints, and inspired the pilgrim to imitate the life of Christ as had the martyred pilgrims that had gone before him.

The veneration of relics and the popularity of pilgrimages had several interesting consequences for church architecture. Relics were first displayed in shrines erected on side altars and niches throughout the main body of the church. As mentioned in the previous chapter,

Church in Isle sur-la-Sorgue, France: This parochial church has survived despite its village being attacked and burned during the French Revolution in 1793 and bombed in 1944 during WWII.

KEY POINT
The addition of the ambulatory and its radiating chapels had a significant effect on the outward appearance of many Romanesque churches. They became perforce a boldly articulated exterior adjunct to the apse.

many Carolingian churches had added reliquary apses that flanked the larger, central apse designed for the altar of the church. Because this arrangement did not accommodate the flow of pilgrims throughout the more popular churches, medieval builders introduced a new element: the crypt. Whereas the early Christian basilicas, such as Old St. Peter's, were built with small tombs beneath the altar, by the ninth century the simple tomb form was also deemed inadequate.

Instead, recalling the catacombs of ancient Rome, passageways fitted with niches were built beneath the sanctuary (and sometimes extended to the transepts or nave), to accommodate the flow of pilgrims to and from the relics and their accompanying shrines that were placed there for veneration by the faithful. Some of the larger crypts were composed of several vaulted aisles, giving them the appearance of small chapels.

The addition of these larger crypts affected the interior of the church. The sanctuary under which the crypt was built was raised above the floor level of the nave. In turn, this new feature helped emphasize the altar as the liturgical climax of the architecture, the place upon which the most important and sacred parts of the Mass took place. At the same time, a natural hierarchy was further emphasized. This arrangement was carried out most notably in Italy, in churches such as San Miniato in Florence (1013), San Zeno Maggiore in Verona (1139), and the Cathedral at Modena (1099), but was not at all uncommon in France and Germany.

Senanque Abbey, Normandy, France: (12th century)

Tarragona Cathedral, Spain: Begun in the 12th century and completed in the 14th, this Spanish cathedral combines elements of both Romanesque and Gothic.

KEY POINT
The addition of larger crypts affected the interior of the church. The sanctuary under which the crypt was built was raised above the floor level of the nave to emphasize the altar as the liturgical climax of the architecture.

Touring St. Martin's

The creation of the ambulatory helped to accommodate the growing number of pilgrims. In this arrangement, the aisles flanking the nave were extended alongside the sanctuary and around the apse. Small relic chapels or niche shrines radiated out from this ambulatory facilitating the flow of pilgrims. The addition of the ambulatory and its radiating chapels had a significant effect on the outward appearance of many Romanesque churches. They became perforce a boldly articulated exterior adjunct to the apse.

The first known ambulatory was designed into the reconstruction of St. Martin in Tours, France. The church was dedicated in 918 with a corridor enclosing the sanctuary to give access to the tomb of St. Martin, located at the head of the apse. A series of round chapels, called absidioles, radiated from the ambulatory, setting the precedent for this new configuration, which was both practical and elegant. In the words of contemporary historian Hans Erich Kubach, the ambulatory is "one of the handsomest achievements of Romanesque architecture. Viewed from the outside, the staggered sequence of absidioles around the ambulatory rising to the dominant projecting apse, itself often surmounted by a crossing tower, creates an unforgettable image." Many of the great pilgrimage churches, such as the Bordeaux cathedral (at right) offer splendid examples.

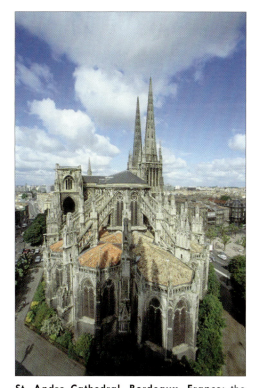

St. Andre Cathedral, Bordeaux, France: the ambulatory and its radiating chapels (seen above) became an identifying characteristic of late Romanesque and Gothic cathedrals.

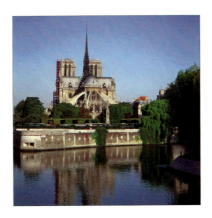

HEIGHT AND LIGHT
Gothic Church Architecture

INNOVATIVE ROMANESQUE ELEMENTS such as the ambulatory and the masonry vault became more common during the early 12ᵗʰ century as the emerging Gothic culture began to leave its mark on the refined Romanesque architecture of the day. During the later decades of the same century, in fact, many Romanesque elements were being transformed into Gothic. The pointed arch, for instance, superseded the semicircular arches of the Romanesque, and the multitude of carved figures used in Romanesque ornamentation were not only used to adorn the vast cavernous portals of Gothic churches, but they were also carved out of supporting columns, giving rise to architectural statuary.

Yet the emergence of Gothic architecture in Europe was not merely the result of a development of

Romanesque forms and the familiar basilican plan. Rather, its emergence owed much to important structural engineering developments that differentiated the architecture of the 12ᵗʰ-15ᵗʰ centuries, as well as to advancements in scholarship, especially during the 13ᵗʰ century.

Looking Up

Influenced by the writings of great thinkers such as St. Thomas Aquinas, Christians began to deepen their spiritual aspiration toward union with God. Even more influential in the area of church architecture, especially in France, was the work of Abbot Suger, who articulated his belief that light, color, richness, and beauty in church architecture should reflect the splendor of God. These beliefs that spread throughout the medieval world were reflected in the overriding characteristic of Gothic architecture: a vigorous verticality that creates a

---

At left: *front facade of the Cathedral of Notre Dame de Rheims in France.*

Milan Cathedral, Italy: (A.D. 1385-1485) Considered the largest Medieval cathedral, the exterior is a gleaming mass of white marble.

heightened sense of aspiration toward God and heaven. Coupled with this was the use of natural light as a means of creating a mysterious, other-worldly feel. Thus, the two distinguishing characteristics wrought by the Gothic language are height and light.

To this end, architects developed an ingenious and innovative structural system that afforded greater ease of vertical construction. The three essential elements of this new method are the pointed arch, the ribbed vault, and the flying buttress. The weight of the building was placed on perpendicular exterior supports called buttresses. These wall-like pillars set outside the church act like slender, gigantic fingers. Since the vertical walls were then free from bearing the weight of the roof, they could be designed with large windows—a marked departure from the relatively small windows used in the design of Romanesque churches.

Growing Panes

Artists normally filled these large openings with panels of

Antwerp Cathedral, Belgium: (A.D. 1352-1411)

Flying buttress, Milan Cathedral, Italy: Wall-like pillars set outside the church, flying buttresses act like slender, gigantic fingers that bear the weight of the building.

stained glass—small pieces of colored glass fit together to form images which told the stories of Jesus and the saints of His Church. Not only was this emerging form of sacred art practical in the sense that it served as a new iconographic element—it taught the dogmas and beliefs of the Church—it provided a way to convert natural light into a colorful heavenly light: When the sun shines through stained glass, the light is transmogrified into beautiful multicolored patterns on the floors inside the church. This strange and unearthly light renders the whole of the interior space heavenly.

Although the stained glass window may ultimately be the most enduring contribution to future church architecture, the new structural system produced many interesting features that facilitated the Gothic church's typically high, lighted interior. In fact, 19th-century architect Viollet-le-Duc contended that 'Gothic' is more a structural system than an architectural style. "Everything is a function of structure," he wrote, "the gallery, the triforium passage, the pinnacle, and the gable; no Gothic architectural form is the result of flights of fancy."

Perhaps the most memorable structural element of the Gothic church is the flying buttress, which varies in shape and size from cathedral to cathedral, yet always serves the same structural purpose. Each is formed by a straight upper surface and a curved lower surface. Heavy spire-topped pinnacles were added on top of the outer pillars in order to properly weigh down the buttress. The presence of the buttress on the exterior of the building not only

KEY POINT
The three essential elements of the Gothic structural system are the pointed arch, the ribbed vault, and the flying buttress.

Antwerp Cathedral, Belgium: Sculptural portals and tympanums are a hallmark of the Gothic language; they owe their origins to their Romanesque precursors.

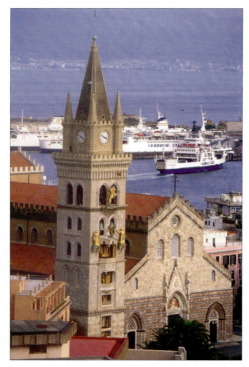

Messina Cathedral, Sicily: (A.D. 1098)

gives the church a certain elegant rhythm, but it also conveys that sense of durability that was effected in earlier church architecture by the use of thick masonry walls.

Practically speaking, the buttress system served to support the church's roof, which was made up of a series of ribbed vaults. The handling of weight and thrust was everywhere facilitated by the use of the pointed arch, which was employed because it allowed the architect to erect a vault over a rectangular space of any size. Yet apart from its structural appropriateness, the pointed arch is well suited to the Gothic language because it emphasizes the verticality of the entire structure, since it points upward unlike the semicircular arches used in Romanesque construction.

The men who designed these innovative structural elements that worked together so well visually and structurally were artists and

KEY POINT
The men who designed these innovative structural elements that worked together so well visually were artists and engineers guided by geometrical concepts of proportion.

St. Elizabeth Church, Marburg, Germany: (A.D. 1233-83)

St. Coleman Church, Cork, Ireland

engineers guided by geometrical concepts of proportion, yet one of the basic methods they used to acquire their technical knowledge was the process of trial and error: They kept at it until they perfected their building techniques. The result was one of the greatest achievements in the history of architecture.

Suger Daddy

Almost all Gothic architects, artisans, and craftsmen remain anonymous to us today. One name, however, is well known to art historians: Abbot Suger, who is credited as being the father of Gothic architecture. His abbey of St. Denis was a small, dilapidated 8th-century building when he reconstructed it between 1130 and 1140 using ribbed vaults and stained glass windows. During that decade, Suger built what is now considered the first Gothic church

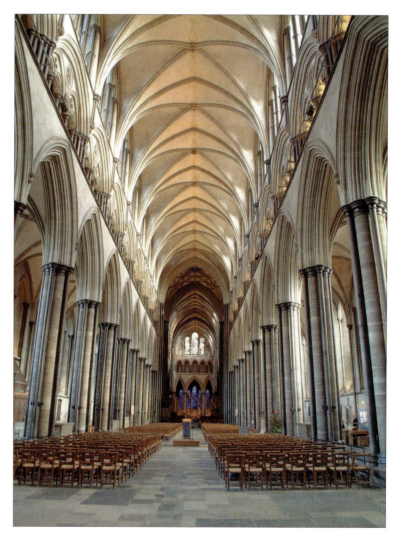

Salisbury Cathedral, England: (A.D. 1220-58)
Characteristic of English Gothic.

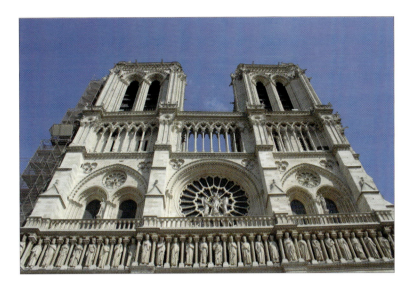

Notre Dame Cathedral, Paris: (A.D. 1163-1235) Characteristic of French Gothic, it served as a model for many later churches built in France.

structure, despite his use of many typically Romanesque features. The influence of the St. Denis reconstruction was felt immediately throughout the Île-de-France. Between 1130 and 1230, 25 cathedrals were built within 100 miles of Paris. The most well-known, of course, is Notre Dame in the capital city. (Almost all Gothic cathedrals in France were placed under the patronage of Our Lady, and therefore bear the name 'Notre Dame.' Other than the cathedral at Paris, they are distinguished therefore by their city name, e.g., Rheims, Chartres, Beauvais.)

KEY POINT
Abbot Suger is credited as being the 'father' of Gothic architecture. He reconstructed his abbey of St. Denis between 1130 and 1140 using ribbed vaults and stained glass windows.

Regional variants

Gothic architecture and its accompanying arts soon radiated out from France to the rest of Europe during the course of the 13th century, taking its various shapes in countries such as England, Germany, Flanders, Italy and Spain.

The Gothic architecture of England is particularly noteworthy for its distinct regional form. Oddly, the English style didn't originate on the British Isles. It was first introduced in northern France before being imported to England in 1174 by Guillaume de Sens via Canterbury Cathedral. Around the same time, the Cistercians monks in the north of England adapted French Gothic building techniques to produce many of the first English Gothic abbeys, most of which now lay in ruins.

Throughout the next several centuries English Gothic architecture passed through three distinct structural styles: First Pointed (1189-

Notre Dame Cathedral, Chartres, France: (A.D. 1194-1260) A popular pilgrimage destination due to its Shrine of the Black Madonna, its south tower (at right) is said to be the most perfect of all Gothic church towers in Christendom.

Ulm Cathedral, Germany: (A.D. 1377-1477) Interior above; at right below, its great western tower and spire, which together rise to 529 feet, making it the tallest church tower in the world.

1307), Curvilinear (1307-77), and Perpendicular (1377-1485). During each of these periods the characteristic structural components (vault, arch, and buttress) were expressed differently. Perhaps the most notable characteristic of the English expression of Gothic architecture throughout all three distinct periods was the uninhibited use of right angles. Instead of a rounded apse, for example, the great cathedrals of York, Ely, Winchester, Salisbury, Lincoln and Wells, all have a rectilinear apse and transepts.

Another distinctly English feature is the use of the open-timber roof, an ornate combination of exposed beams and rafters used throughout England in the construction of parish churches. The most enduring of the open-timber designs is the hammer-beam roof, in which the center of the tie-beams are cut away, and the remaining beam (the 'hammer-beam') is supported by a curved brace attached to the side wall. Both beam and brace are typically decorated. In Germany and surrounding nations of the eastern reaches of the

KEY POINT
One of the most notable characteristic of the English expression of Gothic architecture throughout all three distinct periods was the uninhibited use of right angles.

Siena Cathedral, Italy: (A.D. 1245-1380) The zebra marble striping and elaborately sculptured western facade (pictured here) make this one of the most unusual and most beautiful of Italy's Gothic churches.

Holy Roman Empire there was much opposition to the idea of patterning their architecture after 'imported' Gothic from France, especially in light of their preference here for the use of brick as the primary building material. It was in the late-13th century that German architects combined the new architectonic language with the use of brick (and other masonry units) to produce the distinctively German regional style known as *Backsteingotik*. Some notable examples are St. Elizabeth in Marburg (1233-83, see p. 59), Ulm Cathedral (1377-1477), and St. Stephen's Cathedral in Vienna (1300-1510, at right).

In Belgium, the Gothic churches are characterized by their distinctive towers, spires, belfries and stepped gables, as with the famous Cathedral of Antwerp (1352-1411) with its one immense tower and spire that reach 400 feet (see p. 56).

Due to both climatic and social considerations the Gothic churches in the Mediterranean regions of Spain, Italy, and Sicily developed in a very different manner from their northern counterparts. For one, the conspicuous verticality of northern Gothic was neutralized by the flatness of the roofs and an absence of pinnacles and flying buttresses. The Milan cathedral (1385-1485), however, is one notable exception. In many ways it is more German than Italian in character, although its gleaming mass of white marble is an undeniable regional variant. The cathedrals of Orvieto (1290-1310) and Siena (1245-1380) provide more typical examples of distinctly Italian Gothic churches.

KEY POINT
It was in the late-13th century that German architects combined the new architectonic language with the use of brick (and other masonry units) to produce the distinctively German regional style known as *Backsteingotik*.

St. Stephen's Cathedral, Vienna: (A.D. 1300-1510)

IN THE IMAGE AND LIKENESS OF GOD
The Classical Renaissance

IN ITALY, THE GOTHIC STYLE never really took hold like it did in France, Germany, and England. In a land built on classical antiquity, Gothic was seen as outlandish, alien, and un-Italian. Consequently, Gothic architecture was increasingly regarded with contempt. In fact, the 15th-century Italian architect Filarete (1400-69) once declared: "A curse on those who thought of such rubbish! Only barbarians can have brought it into Italy."

In the next century, these 'barbarians' were called Goths after the Germanic tribes that had sacked Rome one thousand years earlier. Alberti used the term 'Gothic' as a synonym for 'crude' when writing of the architecture we know by the same name; and a few years later Vasari referred to the Gothic as forms to be avoided, calling them 'monstrous and barbarous.'

At left: Il Gesù (A.D. 1568-75), the Jesuit's mother church in Rome, was designed by Vignola.

Rediscovering Antiquity

It was not until the 16th century that the architecture of the pointed arch, rib vault, and flying buttress came to be formally referred to as 'Gothic.' Alberti and Vasari, both pioneering intellects of the Italian Renaissance, saw this medieval architecture merely as a barbaric and unworthy prelude to the rebirth of classical antiquity. From their point of view, the *maniera dei Goti* was antithetical to the sound traditions of ancient Rome that were influencing artists and architects in the 15th and 16th centuries. Yet, the dawning of the Renaissance was not primarily a reaction to the 'barbarous' architecture of previous centuries; it was more a rediscovering of ancient principles that had been nearly forgotten during the previous millennium.

This revival of classical ideals in building and the arts was centered in Florence, but was influenced mainly by the archeological remains still extant in Rome. Filippo

Florence Cathedral, Italy: (A.D. 1296-1462) Filippo Brunelleschi's design of the dome, which spans 138 feet, triumphantly blended a Renaissance dome with a Gothic building.

Brunelleschi's biographer, writing in 1480, relates: "And so he went to Rome, where . . . he observed the ancient way of building and their laws of symmetry. It seemed to him that he could recognize a certain order in the disposition, like members and bones, and it was as though God had enlightened him." The Florentine sculptor and architect had traveled to Rome to study the construction methods of the ancient Romans in order to compete for the commission to design and build the dome of the Florence cathedral (pictured at left and below). Brunelleschi is credited with rediscovering the measurements and proportions of antiquity and first applying these principles to the circumstances of his own day.

With regard to church architecture, his primary aim was to recreate the form of the early Christian basilica, though 'perfecting' it by applying the newly rediscovered mathematical proportions and orders of classical antiquity. The older Christian basilicas were regarded as clumsy and disordered in form. Brunelleschi saw the need to restore the basilica to its ancient perfection. His designs for

Santa Maria del Fiore

San Lorenzo (1425) and Santo Spirito (1436-82), both in Florence, reflected his ideal of the perfected basilican church and provided later generations with a norm.

Body Building

It is most significant that the proportioning system rediscovered by the Florentine architect was based on proportions of the human body. Thus, it was ultimately the human body that informed the arrangement, scale, hierarchy, and proportion of new church architecture during the Renaissance. Vitruvius, a Roman architect writing three decades before the Incarnation, reiterated the Greek understanding of the human body as the measure for all true architecture because it reaffirmed certain mathematical ratios as reflecting the harmony of the universe. To both the Greeks and the Romans of classical antiquity, the Doric, Ionic, and Corinthian orders represented in their proportioning of elements the perfect expression of harmony and beauty. They were seen as a reflection of God's order.

Renaissance artists and architects, influenced by the theories laid down by Vitruvius, reiterated the importance of the human body in material architecture. Leonardo da Vinci's drawing of the 'Homo ad Circulum' and Francesco di Giorgio's 'Vitruvian figure' also express the same appreciation. But it was Vignola, one of the founding fathers of the Baroque, who codified the proportioning

KEY POINT
It was ultimately the human body that informed the arrangement, scale, hierarchy, and proportion of new church architecture during the Renaissance.

Santa Maria Rotunda, Rome: Once a 'pantheon' of heathen deities, it is regarded by many as the most perfect preservation of all buildings of ancient Rome, and served as an architectural guide to Renaissance architects such as Brunelleschi.

St. Peter's Basilica, Rome: (A.D. 1506-1626) Designed and built under the direction of Bramante, Raphael, Michelangelo and Bernini (among others), it is the finest achievement of the Renaissance and has come to represent the mother church of Christendom.

system of the classical orders during the last years of the Renaissance. The resulting architecture was characterized by simplicity, order, and harmony. This fundamental importance of the human form to Renaissance architecture, sharply distinguished it from Gothic.

The greatest Renaissance theorist was Leon Battista Alberti, whose work on Vitruvius (*De re aedificatoria*) was a guiding light to the architects of both his own time and future generations. Alberti's buildings were three-dimensional representations of the theories he laid out. He designed several churches, including two in Mantua (San Sebastiano and Sant'Andrea) which adapted classical temple facades to the needs of Brunelleschi's perfected basilican church.

How Great Their Art

Many remarkable developments during the decades of the 15th and 16th centuries give Renaissance architecture a richness and diversity that is unparalleled in the centuries that preceded it (and arguably in those that came after). The masters of this era produced some of the greatest pieces of religious art and architecture in the history of Christendom. Architects such as Alberti, Vignola, and Michelangelo made insuperable contributions to their own times and to the future development of sacred architecture. Without ignoring or discarding the traditional forms and methods of construction, these trailblazers were aware that they were creating

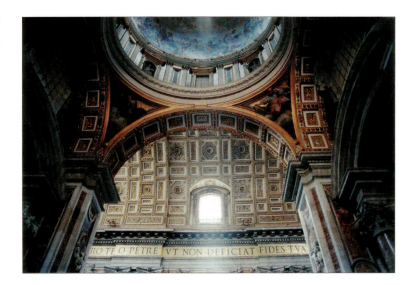

something different—and better.

While the basilican form was the most common classical adaptation for churches during these years, the early Christian form of the martyrion also reemerged. This centralized, domed building used by the ancient Christians to mark the tombs of martyrs became a popular form for Renaissance architects. It is worth noting, however, that in terms of the liturgy they could not properly be considered 'centralized' plans. Following immemorial tradition, the high altar of sacrifice was always placed at the east end of the building and the seating arranged in a unidirectional, linear fashion.

KEY POINT
Without ignoring or discarding the traditional forms and methods of construction, trailblazers such as Alberti, Vignola, and Michelangelo were aware that they were creating something different - and better.

Santa Maria della Salute, Venice: (A.D. 1632) Located on the Grand Canal, this octagonal church adapted the martyrion form of the early Christian centuries.

This square plan was never well suited for the Roman liturgy. Consequently, it was not uncommon for Renaissance patrons to dismiss their architects' martyrium-influenced plans in favor of the longitudinal basilican form. The initial design for the new basilica of St. Peter's, drawn up by Bramante, was based on this Greek-cross arrangement. After Bramante's death in 1516, however, there arose a disagreement as to whether the church should continue to be built in the form of the Greek cross as Bramante had intended or in the shape of a Latin cross as suggested by Raphael, his successor. Some years later Pope Paul V decided to adopt the form of the Latin cross suggested by his new architect Carlo Maderno. Both the Pope and the architect believed this would be more in keeping with early Christian and medieval churches, because this new basilica was destined to become the mother church of Christendom, not simply a martyrium.

Adapting to the human voice

Although the Renaissance is said to have started in Florence with the design of Brunelleschi's cathedral dome, the main centers of architectural progress during the 16th century were Rome and Venice, and it was Bramante's work that would exert the most influence on church design during this period.

A significant work in Rome apart from St. Peter's Basilica, was the mother church of the Jesuits, known as Il Gesù (see p. 64). The church's plan was designed by Vignola around 1568 in consultation with Cardinal Farnese, its patron. In order to accommodate frequent preaching to large congregations, a direct result of the Council of Trent, Vignola designed his plan to be wider and shorter in order to better adapt to the carrying of the human voice.

So successful was Vignola's design of Il Gesù that the church's plan provided one of the most influential models of a Latin-cross church during the Catholic Counter-Reformation, which was just getting underway in Christendom.

Santa Maria della Salute, Venice: (A.D. 1632)

KEY POINT
In order to accommodate frequent preaching to large congregations, a direct result of the Council of Trent, Vignola designed his plan for Il Gesù to be wider and shorter in order to better adapt to the carrying of the human voice.

Our Lady of Kazan Cathedral, St. Petersburg, Russia: Architect Andrei Voronikhin was inspired by St. Peter's Basilica in Rome; this church, in fact, was meant to be a Russian version of St. Peter's and the main church of Russia. After the War of 1812 (during which Napoleon was defeated) the church became a monument to the Russian victory.

AN EMOTIONAL STIMULUS TO PIETY
The Baroque Era

BY THE TIME ST. PETER'S Basilica was completed—during the reign of Pope Clement VIII (1592-1605)—the Catholic Counter-Reformation had inspired a new architectural expression which, while grounded in the Classicism of the Renaissance, was rightly understood as revolutionary in many respects. Carlo Maderno was one of the first architects to break with the prevailing taste for refined Classicism, replacing it with a dynamic architecture that appeared as monumental sculpture. In fact, this sculptural quality is perhaps the most defining characteristic of the 'Baroque,' a term first used in a derogatory sense by 19th-century historians to refer to the arts of the 17th and early-18th centuries. The word owes its origins to the Spanish *barucca*, meaning an unusual pearl of irregular shape.

The churches built during this era, in marked contrast with their Renaissance predecessors, were often irregular in shape. Instead of using the simple geometric forms of Classicism, architects such as Francesco Borromini (1599-1667) used a complex geometry that yielded undulating walls and irregularly shaped spaces.

Going for Baroque

The source of this new expressive style is the Catholic Counter-Reformation inspired by the Council of Trent. In the last session of the Council, in December 1563, the Church reaffirmed the decision made by the Second Council of Nicea regarding the Iconoclasm heresy. The Church proclaimed: "Moreover, let the bishops diligently teach that by means of the stories of the mysteries of our redemption portrayed in paintings . . . the people are instructed and confirmed in faith." This was particularly significant since certain

---

At left: *St. John's Co-Cathedral in Valletta, Malta. Construction began in 1573.*

St. Walburga's Church: (A.D. 1619-43) was the Jesuit church in Bruges, Belgium until 1774. It is now a parochial church.

KEY POINT
The source of the expressive Baroque style was the Catholic Counter-Reformation inspired by the Council of Trent, which ended in 1563.

St. Nicholas Cathedral, Ljubljana, Slovenia

Protestants at the time aimed to destroy religious paintings, statues, and other objects of Catholic devotion.

In the two decades following the close of the Council, churchmen such as Milan's Cardinal Carlo Borromeo recommended that artists and architects respond to the religious concerns expressed by the Council by means of an "emotional stimulus to piety." The net results of this call were churches that integrated architectural elements, sculpture, and painting in order to appeal to the emotions of the faithful and to reassert the dogmas of the faith in a clear and direct way. The subjects of artwork—sculpture, painting, and fresco—included realistic interpretations of biblical scenes as well as dynamic depictions of ecstasies, apparitions, and martyrdoms. Possevino, a lesser known contemporary of Borromeo, encouraged an "unveiled display of truth," writing that even Christ must be

St. Walburga Church, Bruges, Belgium: the subjects of Baroque artwork included realistic interpretations of biblical scenes as well as dynamic depictions of ecstasies, apparitions, and martyrdoms.

KEY POINT
Baroque churches integrated architectural elements, sculpture, and painting in order to appeal to the emotions of the faithful and reassert the dogmas of the faith in a clear and direct way.

portrayed "afflicted, bleeding, spat upon, with His skin torn, wounded, deformed, pale, and unsightly."

Many Baroque churches were erected in order to accommodate the burgeoning new Counter-Reformation religious orders such as the Jesuits and St. Philip Neri's Oratorians. The first of these churches was Il Gesù (p. 64), built in Rome as the mother church of the Jesuits. Its basilican plan reasserted this traditional form as the appropriate one on which a Counter-Reformation architecture should be built. In fact, just a few years later, Borromeo would write, "[The main church in a city] should be a Latin cross plan as, in general, all churches should be."

Seeing Is Believing

St. Ignatius, founder of the society known as the "defender of

Wenceslaus Chapel at the Prague Castle

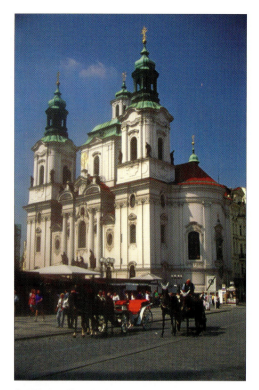

St. Nikolas Church, Prague: Designed by Kilian Ignaz Dientzenhofer, it was completed in 1735. In 1781, after Emperor Jozef II ordered the closure of all churches without a social function, all ornamentation in the church was removed. After a 20ᵗʰ century restoration, the church was given over to the Czech Hussite Protestants.

Cathedral of Cusco, Peru: (A.D. 1560-1664) The façade is very ornamental, and the church contains fine manifestations of colonial Baroque goldsmithing and wood carving.

the Papacy," in his famous *Spiritual Exercises*, stresses the importance of visualizing the subjects of meditation in order to reinforce Christian themes such as the 'four last things': death, judgment, heaven and hell. The first week of Ignatius' 40-day *Spiritual Exercises* is devoted to the contemplation of sin. To this end, he requires the retreatant to see the flames of hell, to smell the sulfur and stench, and to hear the shrieks of the demons. During the last two weeks the retreatant must 'live out' through all the senses the Passion, Resurrection, and Ascension of Christ. The art of many Baroque painters reflects Ignatius' concern with the visual as an aid to contemplation of religious truths. Baroque churches such as Il Gesù sought to do this literally through its building forms and artistic expressions.

Gianlorenzo Bernini (1598-1680), a deeply devout Italian who practiced Ignatius' *Spiritual Exercises*, was undoubtedly the most prolific and influential sculptor of the Baroque period. In addition to his many figural sculptures (e.g., the famous Ecstasy of St. Teresa of Avila), he is credited with the monumental sculptural baldacchino erected beneath the great dome of the new St. Peter's Basilica as well as its Cathedra Petri, the Chair of Peter located in the apse.

Innovative Elements

Despite Bernini's acclaim and numerous accomplishments, it was his contemporary, Borromini, who was the greatest of the Baroque architects. He, as few others could, drew both upon his knowledge of Classicism and his technical understanding of Gothic construction

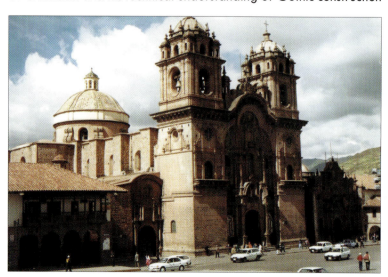

Church of Our Lady of Succor, Graz, Austria: Built for the Minorite brothers, this church sits on the right bank of the Mur River. Pietro de Pomis carried out its reconstruction in the early 17th century, after which it became a popular pilgrimage site.

KEY POINT

The art of many Baroque painters reflects St. Ignatius' concern with the visual as an aid to contemplation of religious truths. Baroque churches sought to do this literally through their building forms and artistic expressions.

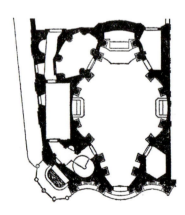

Plan of San Carlo Alle Quatro Fontane

to create such innovative sculptural churches as San Carlo Alle Quatro Fontane, designed for an austere Spanish religious order called the Discalced Trinitarians. The oval plan (at left) surmounted by an oval dome is an interesting interpretation of the basilican layout. Instead of perpendicular angles, the convex and concave walls of the church create an illusion of movement, which is designed to draw the faithful from the outside in and toward the apse and its altar.

Borromini was also adept at using an integrated iconography—painting and sculpture—to express the function and purpose of his churches. He also employed architectural elements such as lanterns placed atop his domes to symbolize the search for wisdom. He sculpted torches to represent the 'light of learning,' and he used stars, crossed palm leaves, and winged cherub heads to refer to eternal life.

Although centered in Rome, where all Borromini's great works can be found, the Baroque architecture of Italy influenced the design of churches throughout much of Catholic Europe and even as far as the Spanish and Portuguese colonies of South America. Characterized by flamboyant, expressive and very colorful decor and facades, the colonial Baroque churches have long been an integral part of the spirituality of South and Central American Catholicism.

Peru and Mexico were the two main centers of colonial Baroque church architecture, but no part of Central or South America was untouched by the influence of the Spanish missions. A unique mixture of Spanish and native elements, this Baroque-inspired style flourished in the New World until the late-18th century. Elaborate and intricate ornamentation with large, curvy forms was typically coupled with simple, solid construction to produce many ecclesiastical gems that predate the churches of North America by centuries. Perhaps the most important colonial church is that of the cathedral in Mexico City (below) with its richly carved columns and entablatures as well its dramatic alternations of curves and angles.

As in Spain, the opulent style known as Churrigueresque (named after Spanish architect Jose Benito Churriguera) was popular for some time in the Spanish colonies. The term typically refers to the

San Carlo Borromeo Church, Noto, Sicily: The historic center of this Sicilian village is almost entirely composed of Baroque buildings, including San Carlo Church, which dates from the early 1700's.

KEY POINT
Although centered in Rome, the Baroque architecture of Italy influenced the design of churches throughout much of Catholic Europe and even as far as the Spanish and Portuguese colonies of South America.

Mexico City Cathedral, Mexico: Built mostly between 1573 and 1667, it is the largest and oldest cathedral in the Americas.

capricious use of Baroque motifs and extreme richness and exuberance in the sculptural decoration of churches (see bell tower at right).

Bell tower, Santa Prisca Church, Taxco, Mexico: (below) Architects of the Baroque often used expressive sculptural iconography in exterior facades, as in this bell tower below.

Overwrought rock-work

In 1620, as part of the Catholic Counter-Reformation, Protestantism was outlawed in Austria. This, in turn, sparked the revival of church architecture as an art form in the Catholic community. Although influenced by Borromini and other accomplished Italian architects of the period, the Baroque churches of Austria took on their own unique characteristics.

Salzburg was the first center for this Austrian revival as dramatic, theatrical churches such as the reworked Church of Our Lady of Succor (see p. 78) were constructed throughout the 17th century. Architect Santino Solari was 'imported' from Italy to design Salzburg's cathedral. His design, with its large dome, rounded transepts and Latin cross plan, was inspired by the Baroque churches of Rome, especially St. Peter's, though it is worth noting that the

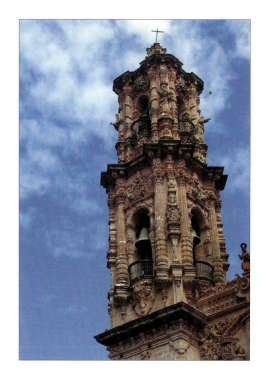

Graz Cathedral, Austria: The church was originally designed in the 12th century as a Romanesque structure, but was later expanded in a Gothic manner and, in the 18th century was remade in the Baroque.

St. Peter's Church, Munich: The oldest church in Munich, it was remade in the Rococo style during the late 17th and 18th centuries.

church was uniquely Austrian in expression. No one was going to mistake it for a Roman church.

The first Austrian-born Baroque church architect was Johann Bernhard Fischer von Erlach, who trained with both Bernini and Borromini in Rome. As the foremost exponent of Austrian Baroque, his two greatest church accomplishments were Salzburg's Trinity Church and the Karlskirche in Vienna.

In Germany, because of the Thirty Years War and other political upheavals, Baroque architecture didn't flourish there until the 18th century. By the latter part of that century, the Rococo style was grafted onto Baroque architecture in both Austria and Germany. The term, derived from the French *rocaille,* meaning 'rock-work,' was applied to the ornate progression of Baroque, the ornamentation of which was purposefully pushed to extremes. Its hallmarks included gilt and ornate stucco, brightly colored frescoes, arabesque ornamentation, elaborate curves and asymmetry.

The interiors of churches such as St. Peter's in Munich and Melk Abbey in Lower Austria seemed to almost drip with their Rococo embellishments, so much so that Rococo came to be seen as synonymous with decadence and overwrought lavishness.

Moreover, the churches designed in this brief era are characterized by an overblown flamboyance that most people today would consider gaudy or even ugly. Nevertheless, the Baroque era produced some of the finest churches of Christendom, which continue to be popular pilgrimage sites to this day.

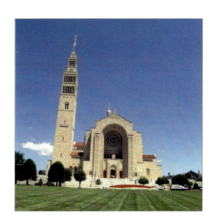

LEARNING FROM THE PAST
The Revivalist Movements

IT WAS THE OVERWROUGHT ornamentation and pompous theatricality of the Rococo churches that encouraged the Neo-Classical movement of the late 18th and 19th centuries. As early as 1753, architectural theorists such as Abbé Marc-Antoine Laugier were promoting a simplified, rational architecture founded on the 'first principles' of Greek architecture. In the mid-18th century many European architects and artists were being influenced by the rediscovery of Greek temples in Greece and Sicily. The Rococo designs of the Late Baroque period were seen as the antithesis to the simplicity of the ancient Greeks. Thus, a renewed interest in antiquity flowered into Neo-Classicism, which was applied both to religious and secular buildings of the period.

At left: *Sacré Coeur Basilica, Paris: built at the end of the 19th century, its famous form is adapted from Byzantine churches of earlier centuries.*

As regards churches, the exteriors often bore a strong resemblance to Greek temples (with grand Doric porticos, for example), but sometimes with the addition of plain steeple towers. This Greek revival movement was popularized in England, where Sir John Soane was its most prolific and influential exponent. In North America, this Neo-Classicism took many forms. Some imitated the Anglican churches of the British Isles while others were adapted on a much smaller scale to become the Protestant meeting house prototype still common in the landscape of places like New England.

The Historical Smorgasbord

At the same time other so-called revivalist movements were taking root, most notably that of the Neo-Gothic. These Gothic revival churches were criticized for not being properly Gothic but merely Renaissance-like structures dressed up with Gothic

Sacré Coeur Basilica, Paris: built at the end of the 19th century atop Paris' Monmartre.

KEY POINT

In the mid-18th century many European architects and artists were being influenced by the rediscovery of Greek temples. Thus, a renewed interest in antiquity flowered into Neo-Classicism.

features, such as pointed arches, rib vaults and buttresses. Since these traditionally structural elements were not used as structural devices but merely for ornamentation, this faux Gothic was easily criticized as inauthentic, and according to some, influenced the 20th century reactionary movement of architectural Modernism.

The Gothic revival in Great Britain is a notable exception. During much of the 19th century, when Catholics began once again to build public places of worship—it wasn't until 1850 that the Catholic hierarchy was restored to England—the archeologically correct English Gothic revival style, as popularized by A.W.N. Pugin, was the order of the day. The first of Pugin's Catholic churches in London was St. Peter's in Woolwich (1843), followed five years later by Pugin's masterpiece: St. George's Southwark Cathedral (1848).

It was during the 1840's that continental Gothic became more

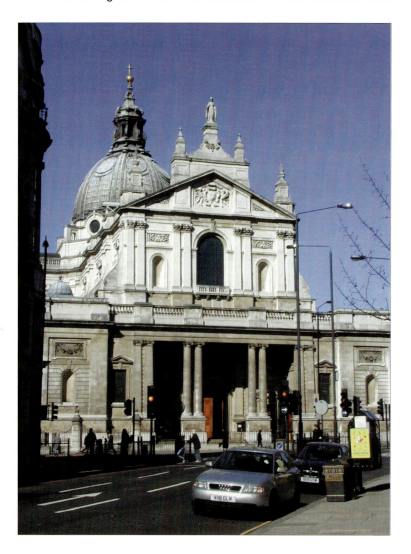

Brompton Oratory, London: built between 1878 and 1896, this Neo-Baroque masterpiece was intended to offer an example to those who were unable to see an Italian church for themselves.

popular throughout Britain, especially in London. One of the finest examples of this style is given by Immaculate Conception Church (1844, see p. 88), a mission parish founded by the Jesuits. The facade, with its arched and gabled central door and tracery rose window, owes more than a passing nod to Beauvais Cathedral's south transept. Its graceful interior, as beautiful as any in England, is richly detailed with carved woodwork and pierced stonework, much of it in marble. Its groin vaulting, pointed arches and reredos point further to its French progenitor. Its twelve chapels and corresponding altars, along with the sanctuary, make Immaculate Conception one of the finest Gothic revival churches in Christendom.

By the late-19th century, the Gothic revival that had taken hold of England was superceded by an historical preference toward a Romanesque and Renaissance revival, rooted in a renewed

Church tower, Brazil

KEY POINT
An indiscriminate 'ecclecticism,' borrowing architectural elements from various styles, resulted in churches that were easily criticized for their lack of harmony.

Brompton Oratory, London: interior view of main altar and sanctuary; most of the furnishings and materials were imported to London from Italy.

Immaculate Conception Church, Mayfair, London: One of the finest examples of the 19th century Gothic revival in England. Its graceful interior is richly detailed with carved woodwork and pierced stonework, much of it in marble. Its groin vaulting, pointed arches and reredos point further to its Gothic roots.

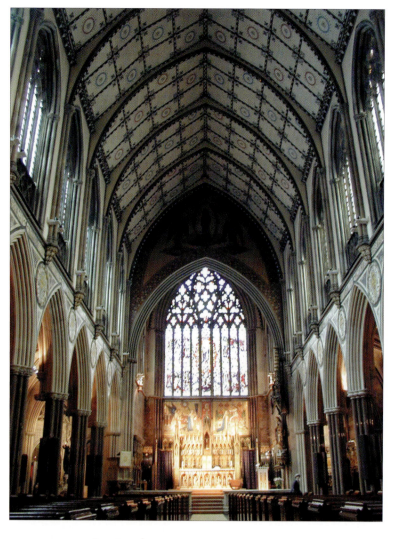

KEY POINT
The Counter-Reformation era solidified the universal use of church furnishings such as pews, kneelers, communion rails, ornate pulpits, side aisle shrines, stained glass windows, and candles.

appreciation of Italian architecture.

The Italian Renaissance style is most fully realized in the Oratory of the Immaculate Heart of Mary on Brompton Road. Built for the Oratorians of St. Philip Neri, introduced to England by Cardinal John Henry Newman, the church is better known as Brompton Oratory (see pages 86-87).

Architect Herbert Gribble was clearly inspired by Il Gesù, the Jesuits' mother church in Rome (see p. 64). Most of the materials, statuary, and artwork that adorn the elaborate interior were imported from Italy. The communion rails, for example, are made of Sicilian and Siena marble, and the baptismal font is a reduced version of that in the Orvieto cathedral.

Although England is renowned for its beautiful historicist churches, the craft was not nearly as well-applied in other places, including in North America. The willingness to look to historical 'styles' of the past, although commendable to a point, had its drawbacks. An indiscriminate ecclecticism, borrowing architectural elements from various styles, resulted in churches that were easily criticized for their lack of harmony; 'inauthentic' use of materials, inappropriately placed statuary and ornamentation, and ill-proportioned architectural elements betrayed a lack of artistic skill and historical understanding.

American Revival(s)

Ultimately, the architects of this period often failed to look to the past *in order to inform their own work*. Rather, they looked to the past in order to duplicate a certain 'look' or 'feel,' but lacked both the technical skill and artistic flair to properly recreate the masterworks of past ages. Consequently, relatively few churches

St. Patrick Church, Soho Square, London: In keeping with the Italianate style, the church was built with a prominent campanile built of red brick in five arcaded stages. One of the facade's most striking features is the portico with its Corinthian columns and pilasters, topped by a carved pediment.

Westminster Cathedral, London: When Cardinal Vaughn decided to build a new Catholic cathedral in London, he was careful not to consider a Gothic inspired scheme because he wanted to avoid detrimental comparisons with the Anglican's Westminster Abbey. Architect J.F. Bentley was inspired instead by the Byzantine churches of northern Italy.

Altos de Chavon Church, Dominican Republic: Built high above the Chavon River, this 16th century-style Mediterranean village was created by hand in the 1970's out of stone, iron and wood.

KEY POINT
Swift-changing fashions and a break with the history and tradition of church design produced the banal and uninspiring religious buildings of the 20th century.

of this era can be considered works that will generously inform the work of future architects. There are, however, some notable exceptions such as the Gothic-inspired St. Patrick's Cathedral in New York City and Sacred Heart Basilica in Newark, New Jersey. St. Matthew's Cathedral in Washington, D.C. (see p. 85), completed in 1893 in the mode of the northern Italian Renaissance, was cruciform in plan with a large dome over its crossing. It inspired the use of revivalist styles other than the Gothic, which was by far dominant in the U.S. in the late 19th-century.

There were also some prolific American architects who are notable for their exceptional skill and artistry, for example, H.H. Richardson, the father of the heavily rusticated American Neo-Romanesque and Ralph Adams Cram, a High Anglican who favored the Gothic.

Cram was also a prolific theorist and lecturer who was often pressed to defend his reliance on architectural tradition and history. In his seminal work *Church Building* (1899) he responded with this memorable point:

"And above all else, let us remember this: when we build here in America, we are building for now, we are manifesting the living Church. It is art, not archeology, that drives us. *From* the past, not *in* the past. We must return for the fire of life to other centuries, since a night intervened between our fathers' time and ours wherein the light was not; and therefore it does not come direct to our hand."

No architect of the early 20th-century perhaps better epitomizes the American revival in Catholic church architecture than Edward J. Schulte, an under-recognized master church builder whose works include cathedral churches in La Crosse, Cincinnati, and Lexington. During the boom years of 1915-1965, an extraordinary number of churches were built in the United States. Schulte was responsible for over one hundred of them during his long career. Though not known as an architectural innovator, he was adept at looking to the past in order to design for the present and the future. His church designs reflect his deep understanding of and obvious appreciation for the history of Catholic church building.

San Nicolas Church, Cali, Colombia: (19th century)

Mission style church, Florida

KEY POINT
The basilica plan, confirmed by universal adaptation throughout all Christian centuries, continued to be used in the design of almost all Catholic churches during the 19th and 20th centuries.

La Ermita Church, Cali, Colombia: (A.D. 1926-1942) Dedicated to Our Lady of Sorrows, this Neo-Gothic church design was inspired by Germany's Cologne Cathedral.

KEY POINT
The Spanish mission churches of the western United States and the richly-styled Mexican churches of the late 19ᵗʰ century were descendents of the Baroque model in facade, the arrangement of spaces, and the ornamentation used.

Descendents of the Baroque

Although many churches built or reconstructed in the late-18ᵗʰ and 19ᵗʰ centuries reflected a reaction to Late Baroque flamboyancy and its lack of self-restraint, the earlier strain of Baroque (the churches that grew out of the Counter-Reformation) continued to influence church architecture in the New World well into the 20ᵗʰ century.

The Spanish mission churches of the western United States and the richly-styled Mexican churches of the late 19ᵗʰ century, for example, were direct descendents of the Baroque model in façade, the arrangement of spaces, and the ornamentation used. The greatest influence effected by the Baroque architecture of Rome was its integration of sculpture, painting, architectural detailing, and form. This masterful integration produced the high altars and reredos (the sculptural piece behind the altar that usually contains paintings and statues) so common to New World churches built in the late-19ᵗʰ and early-20ᵗʰ centuries.

By the time that Revivalist movements were growing around the globe there was more or less universal use of church furnishings such as pews, kneelers, communion rails, ornate pulpits, side aisle shrines, stained glass windows, and candles. It is worth adding that all of these individual elements were introduced centuries earlier. Furthermore, the basilica plan, confirmed by universal adaptation throughout all centuries of Catholic church architecture, continued

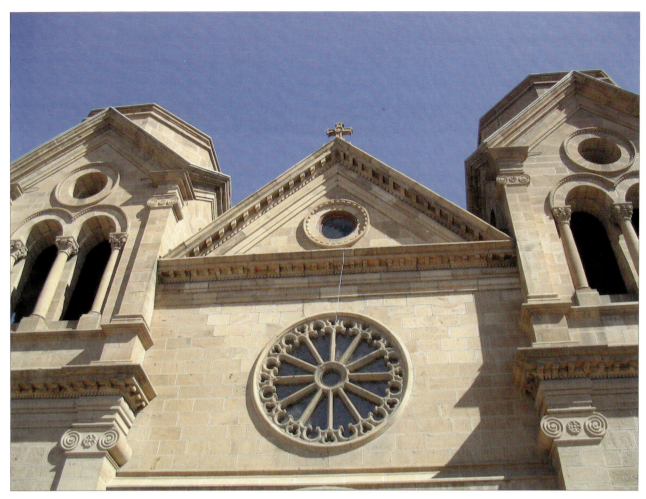

to be used in the design of almost all *Catholic* churches during the 19th and 20th centuries.

St. Francis Church, Santa Fe, New Mexico: (20th C.)

Tradition and innovation

Perhaps no better example of synthesizing history and tradition with innovative design and modern technology can be rendered than that of Spanish architect Antoni Gaudi's Sagrada Familia in Barcelona. Unlike Cram, Richardson or Schulte, Gaudi (1852-1926) was recognized as one of the most innovative architects of the late-19th and early-20th century. He also earned the nickname 'God's architect' due to his belief that God was ultimately his client on this grand church project.

Gaudi, known as a 'neo-medieval nationalist' in his day (and consequently loathed by the anti-Catholic Spanish Communists), developed a unique personal style of building, one that has become a defining element of the Barcelona landscape. To many

KEY POINT
Gaudi's masterpiece resembles the great cathedrals of the medieval age. Sagrada Familia was based on the plan of a Gothic basilica with a large nave, four transepts, and an apse with an encircling ambulatory.

St. John Cathedral, Savannah, Georgia: (A.D. 1896-1920) Inspired by French Gothic precursors, it is a typical North American expression of Neo-Gothic.

Catalonians, in fact, Barcelona *is* Gaudi. His work is characterized by the use of naturalistic forms, and his approach came to be known as the 'biological style,' a striking interpretation of the continental Art Nouveau movement.

True to form, Sagrada Familia is known for its conical spires, parabolic arched doorways, convex vaults, and freely curving lines. As in most of his work, Gaudi created the impression that the stone used was soft and modeled like clay or wax, producing that sculptural quality that so characterizes his work. Critics have described the church as a "fabulous riot of fantasy." At the same time, Gaudi's masterpiece resembles the great cathedrals of the medieval age. Sagrada Familia was based on the plan of a Gothic basilica with a large nave, four transepts, and an apse with an encircling ambulatory.

Sagrada Familia, Barcelona, Spain: Architect Antoni Gaudi's magnum opus, the 'Temple' as it is known, was begun in 1882 and is still under construction today.

Belfry: tower of Sagrada Familia, Barcelona, Spain

Cathedral Basilica of St. Louis, Missouri

Gaudi himself directed the construction of the church from 1883, when he was 31, until his untimely death in 1926. Although he began work on the church with a purely architectural interest, lacking any religious conviction, in the course of the next 43 years he developed a deep passion for the church. He came to regard Sagrada Familia as a great mission. He became so involved with the church that he set up residence in his on-site studio and devoted the final 14 years of his life to this most important of all his projects. During those years, in his work as an architect, he considered himself obligated to no one but God, whom he referred to as the 'master builder.'

With Sagrada Familia, the inspired architect wanted to create a truly '20th-century cathedral,' a synthesis of all his architectural knowledge, using a complex system of Catholic symbolism and a visual explication of the mysteries of faith. He designed facades representing the Nativity, Crucifixion, and Resurrection of Christ. He also wanted to give the edifice a spectacular vertical dimension by way of an effusion of pinnacles. To that end, he designed eighteen towers—more than any church in Christendom—symbolizing the twelve apostles, the four evangelists, Christ, and the Virgin Mary. The tallest of these, the Christ tower, will stand some 500 feet when it is completed. To date, eight of the eighteen towers are completed. Each was built as a unique spiral shape covered in patterns of Venetian glass and mosaic tiles crowned by the Holy Cross (for detail, see p. 95).

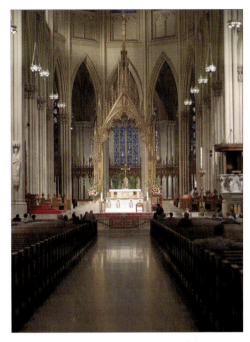

St. Patrick's Cathedral, New York City: (A.D. 1858-1931) Designed by American architect James Renwick, it is the largest Gothic-inspired Catholic church in the United States (exterior facade pictured below).

KEY POINT
With Sagrada Familia, the inspired architect wanted to create a truly '20th-century cathedral,' a synthesis of all his architectural knowledge, using a complex system of Catholic symbolism and a visual explication of the mysteries of faith.

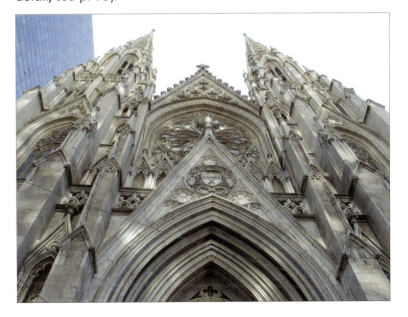

St. Patrick's Cathedral, New York City

BREAKING WITH THE PAST
The Advent of Modernism and the Return of Iconoclasm

BEGINNING IN THE MID-19th century, low-church Protestants began experimenting with a variety of forms and configurations in church design that departed dramatically from the historical precedents of previous centuries. There were several reasons for this experimentation. First, a Protestant revisionist movement flowing from the Rhineland understandably sought to distance itself from the long-held traditions of the Catholic Church. Ever since the Reformation, Protestants had differentiated themselves from their Catholic co-religionists by emphasizing their differences in belief and in worship. But, by and large, it was not until the 19th century that these differences were fully expressed in built form.

For the first time, Christians turned away from the traditional basilica and martyrium models in favor of

---

At left: *The abstracted forms of crucifix and spire of a late-20th century church in New Zealand.*

secular precedents: houses, Greek amphitheaters and auditoria. These churches were configured to center on the power of the preacher rather than on the altar as Ralph Adams Cram was advocating at the time. Tradition was turned inside-out—and for a purpose. The Protestant liturgical movement recognized the necessity of an architecture that reflected its idiosyncratic theology, even if that meant this architecture would be consciously non-ecclesial—without altar, tabernacle or sanctuary.

By the turn of the 20th century, the noted architects of the day were producing church designs with the first tenet of Modernism in mind: the need to break with the past in order to create a so-called 'new architecture for modern man.' Architects such as Frank Lloyd Wright masqueraded as theologians in order to produce church designs that were little more than conduits for their own architectural and ideological

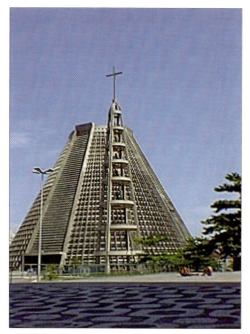

Sao Sebastiao Cathedral, Rio de Janeiro, Brazil: (A.D. 1964) The quasi-conical form has no historical precedent in Christendom. Rather, its precedent is the Mesopotamian ziggurat, the most famous of which was the Tower of Babylon.

idiosyncrasies. Historical styles and elements in church architecture were to be rejected in favor of abstracted designs that glorified man and technology.

Wright's Unity Temple (1904), for example, was designed as a barren auditorium; Louis Sullivan's St. Paul United Methodist Church (1914) was conceived as an abstracted Roman theater; and during the 1920's, Germany's Otto Bartning designed some of the first churches-in-the-round that would later become so popular throughout Western Christendom. These name-brand architects, and others like them, were the trend-setters of their day; they were also successful architects inasmuch as their new churches truly did reflect the reductionist views of the clients they served.

Cold and barren

Unfortunately, many of these new theories of architecture, theology, and liturgy (inspired by both Protestantism and Agnosticism) increasingly affected the Catholic Church through the course of the 20th century. After the Second World War, Catholics also began experimenting with new forms and configurations despite the fact that the Protestant novelties were not fitting expressions for the Catholic Church, her worship, her creed, or her traditions. Some of this experimentation was inspired by the Catholic liturgical movement driven by patrons of Modernist art and architecture such

KEY POINT
Many new theories of architecture, theology and liturgy (inspired by both Protestantism and Agnosticism) increasingly affected the Catholic Church through the course of the 20th century.

St. Aloysius Gonzaga Church, Cincinnati, Ohio: (A.D. 1958) This parochial church-in-the-round is an excellent example of the progressive fad in which architects were inspired by the imagined forms of space travel. This lunar landing module design was popular in the late 1950's and early 1960's. This form quickly went out of style once the U.S. put a man on the moon.

Most Holy Trinity Church, Vienna: (A.D. 1974-76) Designed by sculptor Fritz Wotruba, the exterior walls consist of 152 modular cubes cast in concrete and arranged in an irregular pattern. This is an excellent example of a church that consciously breaks with history and tradition, rendering itself meaningless.

as the Benedictines in North America and the Dominicans in Europe. Iconography was shunned, the basilica arrangement was discarded, and the sacred was no longer distinguished from the profane. Using hard lines and abstracted geometries, architects such as Rudolph Schwartz and Dominikus Bohm created cold, barren 'worship spaces' long before this experimentation reached its height in the decades following the Second Vatican Council (1962-65).

This experimentation, however, was more inspired by the architectural fads of the day: those that were rooted in the International Style, a mode of design in which the architect willfully disregards both space and time. Following Modernist thinking, the architectural fruits of such a theory would be as much at home on the white cliffs of Dover as in the valley of the deepest crater on the moon. History no longer mattered. Geography, topography, culture and climate were no longer considerations. Consequently, the churches designed according to this ideology singularly failed to serve as vessels of meaning. Instead, the Modernist churches were structures that were little more than monuments to their designers—or in some cases, monuments to their patrons.

Two of the finest examples of this ideology are illustrated by Swiss architect Le Corbusier. His Notre Dame du Haut in Ronchamp, France (right) is perhaps the epitome of a church designed as abstract sculpture (though he would later be rivaled by sculptor-architects such as Fritz Wotruba, see photo above). Le Corbusier's Dominican monastery at La Tourette, though critically acclaimed by

KEY POINT

Using hard lines and abstracted geometries, architects such as Rudolph Schwartz and Dominikus Bohm created cold, barren 'worship spaces' long before the Second Vatican Council (1962-65).

Notre Dame du Haut, Ronchamp, France: (A.D. 1956) Designed by Le Corbusier, it is considered to be the epitome of a church designed as abstract sculpture.

Modern church, Belgium: (late 20th century)

KEY POINT
One of Le Corbusier's most significant contributions to the canons of architectural Modernism was his belief that the machine, not the human figure, was the paradigm for architecture.

Abstracted and mottled: An appreciation for beauty was replaced in many places with a license for novelty, which often translated into banality, ugliness, or (as in the case of this stained glass) both.

the architectural establishment, was such a monumental failure with its barren, oppressive spaces that it was forced to close. Le Corbusier succeeded, however, in paving the way for further missteps in Catholic church design for decades to come. He inspired the misguided belief that a man of no faith could be an ideal designer of a church, forgetting that the church was to serve a population that held a certain set of beliefs, worshiped in a particular rite, and was part of a culture that identified strongly with both history and tradition.

From man to machine

One of Le Corbusier's most significant contributions to the canons of architectural Modernism was his belief that the machine, not the human figure, was the paradigm for architecture. He famously stated that "a house is a machine for living." This canon was duly applied to Catholic church architecture in the 1960's as the Church, misguided as she was by the noveau liturgical movement, bought into the idea that new church architecture should exploit modern building materials and methods. Thus, most products of this age were created from steel, glass, and reinforced concrete, designed as hulking masses in the shape of seashells, sailboats, arks, and other nautical themes; ziggurats, rocket ships, beehives, teepees, lunar landing pods, and various shapes of origami.

Even after the architectural establishment offered a well-publicized critique of Modernism, the Catholic Church (through the heavy-handed liturgical establishment) continued to cling to the Modernist ideologies, creating a sort of archi-liturgical culture war. Church reformers after the Second Vatican Council continued to experiment with new forms and configurations in church design in an effort to distance Catholics from the traditional beliefs and practices of their faith. Like their Protestant predecessors of the 19th century, they understood the power of the built environment—its ability to influence the human person.

Reductionist sculpture

In short, by applying the principles of Modernism to Catholic church architecture, architects and patrons (bishops and priests, in most cases) failed to address the relationship between the built form and Catholic faith, theology, and worship. This fact was excellently illustrated at the end of the 20th century through three prominent international architecture competitions to design churches for the 21st century and beyond.

In 1995, the Diocese of Rome sponsored a well-publicized competition to design what it called a 'Jubilee Church' in a working-class suburb of Rome. With the implicit blessing of Pope John Paul II, the diocese invited six of the most widely-acclaimed architects in the world: Tadao Ando from Japan, Santiago Calatrava from Spain, Gunter Behnisch from Germany, and Peter Eisenman, Richard Meier, and Frank Gehry from the United States. A jury made up of clerics and architects chose the design of Richard Meier, a New York architect known for his sparkling white steel-paneled museum designs such as L.A.'s billion dollar J. Paul Getty Center.

Meier's winning design, which was later completed in 2002, is notable for its lack of connection with the life of the Church over the past two thousand years. Meier, a man of admittedly little faith (although Jewish by birth), prided himself on the fact. Acknowledging that he was inspired by Le Corbusier's Ronchamp chapel and La Tourette monastery, he was quoted widely as stating the obvious, that his church was not a traditional design: "If the Diocese of Rome

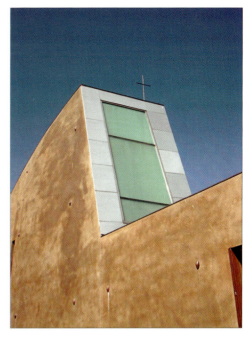

Chapel of St. Ignatius, University of Seattle: (A.D. 1997) Described by architect Stephen Holl as "a stone box containing seven bottles of light," the architectural language used is decidedly abstract and universal.

Millennium Church of the Great Jubilee, Rome: (A.D. 2000) The fruit of a competition for the so-called 'Jubilee Church' of the Roman suburbs, American architect Richard Meier's white concrete 'sails,' glass ceilings and skylights make this church an iconic landmark of contemporary architecture.

KEY POINT
By applying the principles of Modernism to Catholic church architecture, architects and patrons failed to address the relationship between the built form and faith, theology and worship.

Los Angeles Cathedral, California: (A.D. 2000-2002) Designed by Spanish architect Raphael Moneo, it is commonly referred to as the 'Rog Mahal' and the 'Taj Mahony' after the cathedral's patron Roger Cardinal Mahony.

KEY POINT

Architect Richard Meier made a telling comment when he won the competition to design the Jubilee Church of Rome: "If the Diocese of Rome wanted a traditional church, they would not have asked me to participate in the competition."

Millennium Church of the Great Jubilee, Rome

wanted a traditional church, they would not have invited me to participate in the competition."

Meier's Jubilee Church, which is said to be conceived by the Diocese of Rome as a prototype for the Third Millennium, is a reductionist sculpture featuring a series of curvilinear and rectilinear concrete walls infilled with glass, all placed on a horizontal white plinth as if the building could be dug up some day and transported to any other vaguely horizontal surface on the face of the earth. Many critics have commented that Meier's design pays tribute more to the Sydney Opera House than any church building. Its interior is a fragmented, asymmetrical space in which every element is bifurcated by another object. One critic characterized the design as a "perfectly puritanical Reformation space." As such, the design is a success when evaluated as a piece of architectural Modernism. When evaluated as a Catholic church, however, Meier's design falls woefully short, having more to do with his own self-expression than with any understanding of history, tradition or ritual in the Catholic Church. Ultimately, the Jubilee Church is a monument to Richard Meier.

Concrete monstrosity

The second prominent church design competition was held in Los Angeles. Here too, six prominent architects (including Calatrava and Gehry again) were invited to submit designs for the new

Cathedral of Our Lady of the Angels. As with the competition in Rome, none of the architects was known as a designer of religious structures, nor was any known to be particularly religious. In this competition Spanish architect Jose Raphael Moneo emerged victorious.

Lauded as a "landmark of remarkable intelligence" by some and derided by others as a "concrete monstrosity," most public critics evaluated the new Los Angeles cathedral, completed in 2002, according to the canons of modernist architecture—i.e., what the building says about itself. The cathedral is decidedly abstract and modernist in its architectural vocabulary. With its hulking shape, sharp-edged profile, asymmetrical layout and unsettling lack of right angles, this church building also consciously breaks with the historical continuity of two millennia of Catholic church architecture. Instead it pays homage to the past fifty years of banal and uninspiring utilitarian office structures that have littered the landscape of downtown Los Angeles and most other American cities. Rather than acknowledging the greatness of the Church's architectural patrimony and manifesting the permanence of the faith that it serves, Our Lady of the Angels springs from the fashions of the day and the whims of its designer. The cathedral is devoid of any sign value both in its form and in its details. It signifies nothing beyond itself. That may be an interesting intellectual experiment in

Interior, proposed design for Oakland Cathedral, California: (A.D. 2000).

KEY POINT
L.A.'s new cathedral pays homage to the past fifty years of banal and uninspiring utilitarian office structures that have littered the landscape of downtown Los Angeles and most other American cities.

Oakland Cathedral, California: This proposed design by Santiago Calatrava was the winner of a high-profile competition for a new cathedral in Oakland, California. It was later scrapped by the Diocese of Oakland for unspecified reasons.

St. Mary's Cathedral Basilica, Covington, Kentucky: Lay Catholics gathered together on the steps of this cathedral in 1999 to protest the proposed renovation of this Neo-Gothic church. The proposed plans included removing the baldacchino, 17 statues and the ornate sanctuary woodwork.

St. John's Church, West Chester, Ohio: Typical mundane church design dating from the 1990's, when the trend in Catholic church architecture was to make the church building look like anything but a church: doctor's office, nursing home, library, gym club, public school, etc.

formalism, but it doesn't exactly beckon souls from afar. In fact, little of the building's form indicates that it is indeed a church. Instead of a beacon on a hill, the Los Angeles cathedral restricts itself to being a kind of sculptural mass.

Moneo also avoided the use of architectural elements—windows, columns, arches, buttresses, or arcades—that have been the identifying hallmarks of church architecture throughout all previous epochs. His purist palette did not allow it. In addition to jettisoning history, Moneo also dismissed the current culture and *genius loci*. Despite the fact that the architect was a Spaniard designing a cathedral for a diocese that is largely Hispanic, neither his abstract vocabulary nor his utilitarian design reflect a grounding in Spanish culture (as did L.A.'s previous cathedral), which would be most fully manifest in Mission-style architecture, beloved in California, of colorful icons, sacred imagery and organic forms. Instead, Catholics in Los Angeles will be worshipping and praying in a cold box with its modernist pure forms, hard lines, distressing angles and asymmetry. As with Meier's Jubilee Church, the Cathedral of Our Lady of the Angels is about itself and its architect.

Independent of the Church

The third prominent church design competition took place in Oakland, California. Again, six internationally-acclaimed architects were invited to compete for a cathedral commission. This time Spanish-born architect Santiago Calatrava (who had also competed in the previous two competitions) was awarded the project. Calatrava, an accomplished engineer and designer of bridges and pavilions, applied his penchant for bone-like structures to sacred architecture. His proposed design for the Christ the Light Cathedral was likened to a giant clam shell, a rib cage, and the belly of a whale. It was also the first cathedral designed with a retractable roof.

Less cynical critics likened the cathedral's form with its great upward-arching vertebral seam to "a miter with a hat brim," or hands joined in prayer. The *San Francisco Chronicle* described the proposed church as "a rib-like armature of painted steel, glass, and concrete that seems as much futuristic as the skeletal remains of a hunched prehistoric creature."

The form of the building, however, is less remarkable than the architect's theory upon which his design is based. "Since Oakland is home to many different cultures," Calatrava told the *Chronicle*, "my ambition is to give Oakland's cathedral a universal character independent of the Catholic Church." Denying the possibility of a Catholic culture that transcends time and place, his aim was to create a Taj Mahal, "a monument to love in all cultures."

Few will argue that Calatrava was unsuccessful in achieving his desired aim. His design for Christ the Light Cathedral is most certainly independent of the Catholic Church—its agnostic aesthetic embraces no particular doctrine, and its form, to be achieved only by brilliant feats of structural gymnastics (a Calatrava trademark), is reflective neither of Catholic tradition nor architectural history.

Avoiding meaning

For reasons not yet publicly known, Calatrava's design was later dropped by the Diocese of Oakland to be replaced by a scheme (unrevealed as of this printing) produced by an architect known for his experience as a designer of American skyscrapers. Nevertheless, the Calatrava design is significant in that Catholic officials in Oakland, as in Los Angeles, held a competition among name-brand architects to achieve the same pan-cultural results, i.e., a secularized and pluralistic 'space' that tips its hat to no particular religion or creed, and places a shorthaired Virgin Mary next to the yin-yang.

Along with the Diocese of Rome, the California dioceses seem to pride themselves on the fact that their 21st century cathedrals will bear little resemblance to churches of past centuries, that Christian iconography will be minimal, and that any symbolism they do use will be more 'universal' than Catholic. One L.A. diocesan official even told the *Los Angeles Times* that its new cathedral "avoids assigning meaning," although in the same breath he begrudgingly admitted that Our Lady of the Angels "obviously will have a certain amount of rhetoric brought into it because it has a certain use."

St. Ambrose Church, Rochester, N.Y.: Jackhammers were a familiar sight in many places during the last three decades of the 20th century. Above, the altar falls victim to a denuding church renovation project.

Church of the Madeleine, Bruges, Belgium: The results of church renovations are not always benign. In the late 1990's this 200-year-old Neo-Gothic church was retrofitted with a 'meditative wading pool' that fills half the nave. The other half of the nave is filled with moveable bar stools in lieu of its former pews.

THE WISDOM OF HINDSIGHT
The Restoration of Catholic Church Architecture

TOM WOLFE, IN HIS SEMINAL critique on Modernist architecture, begins his "From Bauhaus to Our House" essay by pointing out obvious facts that so many people are unwilling to acknowledge. Writing in 1980, he observed that every child now goes to school in a building that looks like a duplicating-machine replacement-parts wholesale distribution warehouse: "Not even the school commissioners, who commissioned it and approved the plans, can figure out how it happened. The main thing is to try to avoid having to explain it to the parents."[1]

The same can be said about the missteps and blunders in Catholic church architecture over the past fifty years. Churchgoers and non-churchgoers alike often ask the same two questions: How and why did these god-awful structures get built in the first place?

At left: (A.D. 2002) Chapel for Thomas Aquinas College in Ojai, California designed by architect Duncan Stroik.

Archbishop Sean O'Malley, speaking to the U.S. Catholic bishops at their national conference in 2000 stated the problem well: "All of us [bishops] have heard the comments of our people frequently, 'this place does not look like a church.' One of the comments that is made is that there's a certain suburbanization of the heavenly Jerusalem that has taken place."

Architectural culture wars

While many Church officials and patrons are still intent on erecting testaments to their own existence, some prominent architects in both North America and Europe are emerging with critiques of contemporary secularized churches. With the wisdom of hindsight, many are waking up to the fact that the 20th-century experiment with church architecture was a monumental failure. Yet the acolytes of experimentation keep

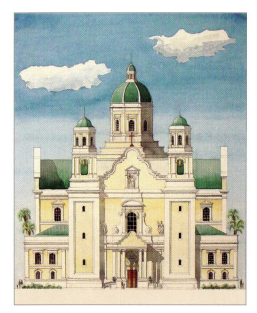

Ave Maria University Chapel: (A.D. 2004) As a student at the University of Notre Dame, Matthew Enquist designed a chapel for a newly founded university in southern Florida.

pressing forward. The result is a sort of architectural culture war.

Liturgical Modernists—they typically embrace architectural Modernism too—are especially distressed by the growing ranks of architects who are embracing the rich history and patrimony of church architecture and building traditions. Michael DeSanctis, associate professor of Fine Arts at Gannon University and a leading light in the contemporary archi-liturgical movement, takes the tradition-minded architects to task. In an editorial published in the *National Catholic Reporter* he calls them "blatant opportunists," "the stodgiest of antiquarians," "recyclers of architectural fashion," and "paranoid and self-righteous Pharisees." He condemns their desire to build upon the rock of history and to eschew the Modernism that has turned church architecture into a carousel of formal experimentation.

The 'traditionalist' architects, from Allan Greenburg and Thomas Gordon Smith in the United States to Francis Roberts, Anthony Delarue and Quinlin Terry in Britain, are simply asking a pertinent question: How can a sense of the sacred be recovered in Catholic church buildings? Part of the answer, they respond, is a return to the emphasis on the 'iconic' nature of building form. In layman's

KEY POINT
Armed with the wisdom of hindsight, church architects of the 21st century are well-placed to learn from the blunders and missteps of recent decades.

Proposal for Ave Maria University Chapel

San Lorenzo Church, Cali, Colombia: (A.D. 2002)

terms, that means the form of the church building has meaning beyond itself; it refers to God, the Church, and her sacraments—i.e., a return to the church as a 'vessel of meaning.'

In projects such as Duncan Stroik's chapel for Thomas Aquinas College (see p. 108) or Anthony DeLarue's Corpus Christi Church in Hertfordshire, England, coherence and unity are hallmarks of these buildings, which are designed using the patrimony of Classical and Medieval architectural languages. Coupled with the restoration of sacred architecture is a revival of Renaissance urbanism—for example, using piazzas, the age-old element of mediation between the Church and the city.

Though it is certainly not necessary to embrace the entirety of Ralph Adams Cram's architectural ideology regarding the role of history in the design of churches, his primary thesis still provides a

Proposal, Clear Creek Monastery, Church of Our Lady, Oklahoma: (A.D. 2002) design and rendering By Matthew Enquist.

helpful point of departure: "We must return for the fire of life to other centuries, since a night intervened between our fathers' time and ours wherein the light was not."[2]

Back to the future

Instead of continuing to lament the degeneration of Catholic church design that characterized the late 20th century, architects, priests, bishops and patrons—all armed with the wisdom of hindsight—are well-placed to learn from the mistakes and blunders of recent decades. The consequences of discarding the successful contributions of the past, both near and distant, are clear. The overwhelming evidence of the day points to the failure of an architecture based on the novelties of Modernism—theological, ideological, and architectural. Yet those involved with producing the sacred churches of the 21st century can learn from the failure of contemporary church design as well as from the noble and successful churches of past epochs.

Church architects and artists especially can draw upon the Scriptural precedents of establishing a 'house of God,' the adaptation of the basilica form by the early Christians, the strength and durability of the Romanesque, the transcendent philosophy of the Gothic, the order and harmony characterized by the Classicism of the Renaissance, the expressive integration of architecture, painting and sculpture from the Baroque, and from an open-minded willingness to look to the past. Without the willingness to learn from

KEY POINT
Architects of our day and age need not and should not build on the unfortunate impoverishment of modern church architecture.

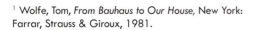

[1] Wolfe, Tom, *From Bauhaus to Our House*, New York: Farrar, Strauss & Giroux, 1981.

[2] Cram, Ralph Adams, *Church Building*, Boston: Marshall Jones Company, 1899.

past mistakes and to study and appreciate the works of past masters, those charged with creating new sacred places will simply perpetuate the crisis in church architecture for years to come.

Ukrainian Catholic Church, New Jersey: (A.D. 2004) design proposal by Dino Marcantonio, Riccardo Vincenzino, and Manuel Mergal.

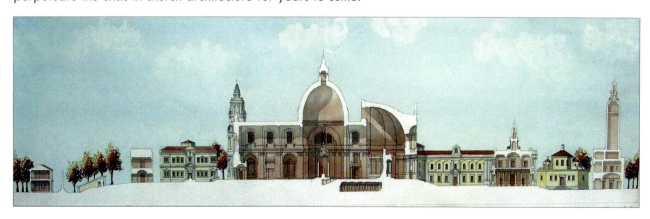

APPENDIX
Glossary of Church Architectural Terms

altarpiece: a painted or carved image or images depicting the dedication of a church (e.g. St. Sebastian, the Annunciation, the Sacred Heart); this is either hung on the wall behind the altar or attached to the back of the altar itself.

altar rail: a low wall, usually balustraded, which distinguishes the sanctuary from the nave; also known as a 'communion rail'; it is here where communicants kneel to receive the Eucharist.

altar stone: a flat, solid piece of natural stone upon which the priest places the Host and Chalice during the Holy Sacrifice of the Mass; it is consecrated by the bishop and marked with five crosses, symbolizing the five wounds of Christ; the altar stone is placed on the surface of the altar.

Colonnade: St. Peter's Basilica, Vatican City

ambo: an elevated lectern used for reading the Scriptures during liturgical ceremonies; traditionally the ambo has a flight of steps on both sides rising to a platform large enough to accommodate the reader and candle-bearers.

ambulatory: a walkway that circumnavigates the sanctuary; originally designed in early pilgrimage churches to enable access to reliquaries and other devotional chapels.

apse: a semicircular extension of the church building; a central apse would serve as the back of the sanctuary.

Apse: The semicircular dome of an apse was often richly decorated with mosaics, frescoes, or reliefs.

Arcade : Campanile, San Marco Cathedral in Venice, Italy

arcade: a row of arches supported on columns, piers, or pilasters and usually roofed; used in church architecture since the early Christian basilicas.

architrave: the beam of the entablature, which extends from column to column.

atrium: an exterior forecourt to a church usually surrounded by a cloister.

baldacchino, baldachin: a permanent ornamental canopy constructed of wood, stone, or metal that is placed over the main altar in a church; it is typically supported by columns.

balustrade: a row of upright supports, usually vase-shaped posts or columns, topped by a rail.

baptistery: a separate building or area of a church containing the baptismal font used for the rite of baptism

basilica: a church that has a long, rectangular nave that leads to a circular apse containing the altar at the head of the structure; the basilica is often extended by transepts that project from the nave.

Holy water font: Brussels, Belgium

Baptistery: Pisa Cathedral, Italy

bas-relief: a sculptural relief that projects very little from the flat background; in a church it is usually carved out of a wall or column.

belfry: the upper room in a tower (campanile) in which bells are hung.

buttress, flying: a projecting arched structure used in Gothic churches such as Notre Dame de Paris to transfer the weight of the roof to the ground; this allows for larger openings in the walls, often filled with stained glass windows.

campanile: a freestanding bell tower made popular by Italian church architecture; it is typically square in plan, although some, such as the famous tower of Pisa, are circular towers.

Campanile: Santa Croce Church, Florence, Italy

cathedra: a bishop's throne in his cathedral church; it is representative of his authority as spiritual head of a diocese.

chancel: the area of the sanctuary reserved to the clergy and servers who are assisting the officiating priest or bishop; usually the front part of the sanctuary nearest the nave.

chapels: places of devotion in a church, usually in honor of a particular saint or for the exposition of the Blessed Sacrament.

Flying buttresses: topped by spire-like pinnacles

Cloister

chevet: a circular or polygonal apse that is surrounded by an ambulatory, usually with radiating chapels.

clerestory: (pronounced "clear-story"), the upper part of the nave walls that usually contains small windows that admit light but no view because of their high placement.

cloister: a covered passageway, usually colonnaded, that encloses a space such as an atrium.

colonnade: a series of regularly spaced columns usually supporting the base of a roof.

column: a vertical support usually consisting of base, shaft, and capital.

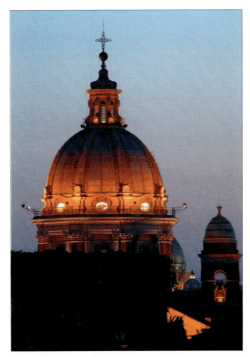
Dome: topped by lantern and cross

cornice: a horizontal, molded projection that crowns a building or a wall.

crossing: the space where the nave crosses the transepts; often capped with a dome.

cruciform plan: a floor plan laid out in the form of a cross; the arms of the cross are formed by projecting transepts.

Dome interior: Santa Maria Maggiore, Rome

crypt: an underground burial place of a saint, typically beneath the altar or the nave of a church.

cupola: a small dome surmounting a roof; or the underside of a dome, the ceiling of a dome.

dome: a half-spherical roof; usually found at the crossing of a church or over chapels.

entablature: in Classical and Neo-Classical architecture, the section of wall that lies between the columns and the roof; it comprises three parts: the architrave, frieze and cornice.

façade: the main face of a church that is usually decorated with religious imagery.

flèche: a slender spire placed over the crossing of a church.

fresco: a wall painting that is executed on freshly spread plaster with water soluble pigments.

gallery: a rear balcony that projects out over the nave.

Cupola and lantern: St. Paul Cathedral, London

Flèche: St. Mary's Cathedral, Sidney, Australia

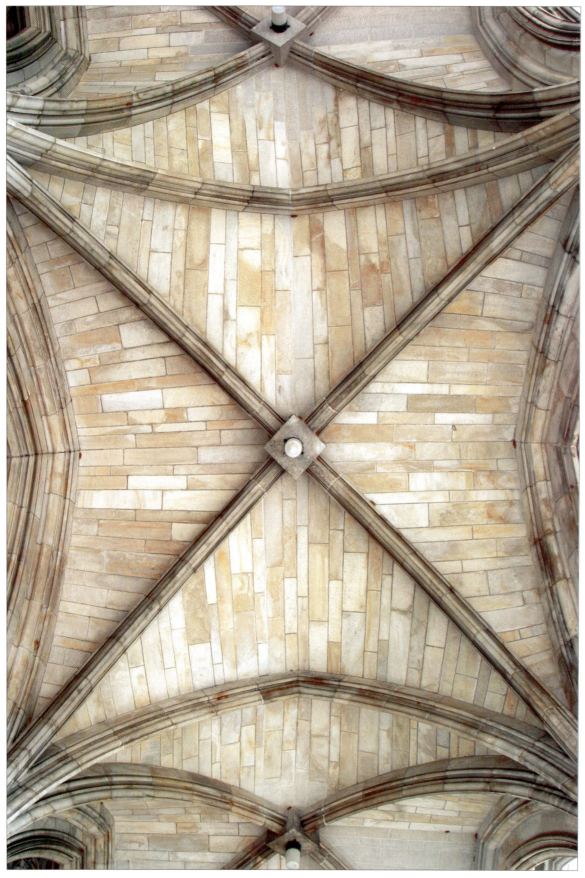

Groin vault masonry

gargoyle: a projecting waterspout, typically designed with grotesque carvings of winged creatures, designed to cast rainwater away from the building.

holy water font (or stoup): a receptacle made of nonporous material for holding holy water.

keystone: the central stone of a semicircular arch, sometimes bearing sculptural bas-reliefs.

lantern: a small tower, usually the uppermost part of a cupola or dome that is used for ornamentation or projecting light; its form often resembles that of a hand-held lantern (see p. 123 and 125).

lintel: the horizontal beam over the head of a doorway; in church architecture the lintel is often used as a decorative surface.

loggia: a gallery behind an open arcade or colonnade.

martyrium, martyrion: a small chapel or church built to commemorate the place where a martyr was killed or buried.

mosaic: a surface decoration made by fitting together small pieces of colored tiles.

Gargoyles: Notre Dame Cathedral, Paris

Mosaic: Chi-Rho symbol of Christ

127

Sculptural pillar: Pisa Cathedral, Italy

narthex: the interior front entrance of a church that serves as a transition from the profane world outside to the sacred space of the church interior.

nave: the main space of a church which accommodates the congregation, it extends from the front entrance to the sanctuary.

niche: a recess in a wall, usually accommodating a statue.

oculus: a round eyelike window or other opening; often found in a central location on the façade above the main doors of a church.

piazza: an open-air plaza of which the church façade serves as a backdrop; the area is used for civic, mercantile, and religious purposes.

Narthex: San Lorenzo Church, Cali, Colombia

pier: a vertical support at either end of an arch.

pilaster: a column, usually rectangular, that projects from a wall.

pillar: a freestanding column that serves as a building support.

pinnacle: a small turret-like spire on top of buttresses, parapets and elsewhere; characteristic of the Gothic language.

Piazza: San Marco, Venice, Italy

Pulpit: Brussels, Belgium

portal: a large opening into a church, or more specifically the decorative area that surrounds the doors.

portico: a covered porch or walkway, usually supported by columns, that leads to the main entrance of a church.

pulpit: an elevated decorative stand in which one preaches; it typically has low walls on all sides except for the entrance from the stairs.

reliquary: a receptacle for sacred relics.

reredos: an ornamental screen of painted panels or carved statues, placed behind and above the main altar in a church; the reredos often contains niches for statues.

retablo, retable: a shelf behind an altar used for supporting decorative works of sacred art, the altar crucifix, and liturgical candles.

rose window: large circular window in the church facade; it is typically made up of different sections of stained glass that resemble the petals of a flower.

shaft: the portion of a column between its base and capital.

Portico: Church of All Nations, Mount of Olives

spire: A tapering tower that crowns a steeple or surmounts the church

steeple: a tower crowned by a spire.

tabernacle: an ornate receptacle, usually on or above an altar, designed to contain the Blessed Sacrament (the Eucharistic host).

tracery: ornamental pattern-work in stone, set into the upper part of a window.

transept: arm-like extensions of the interior of a cruciform-shaped church on either side of the nave near the sanctuary.

triumphal arch: the portion of the wall over the arch that divides the nave from the sanctuary.

tympanum: the area above the lintel of a doorway that is enclosed in an arch; often used for decorative portal sculpture (see below).

vault: an arched covering in stone or brick.

wheel window: a circular window, whose mullions converge like spokes (sometimes used interchangeably with 'rose window')

Steeples and spires: Riga, Latvia

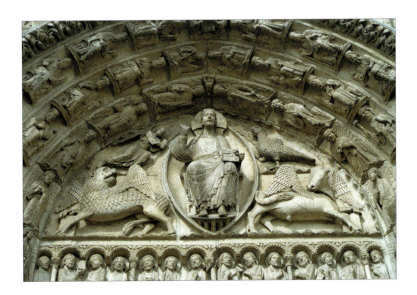

Tympanum: Chartres Cathedral, France

PHOTO CREDITS

page 2: View of Florence Cathedral: Bart Parren

page 5: Church in Perth, Scotland: Andrew Ramsay

page 6: Church in Cuenca, Ecuador: Carlo Ricciardi

page 8: Sandstone church: David Freund

page 9: Church in Horsholm, Denmark: Willem Dijkstra

page 10: Panorama view of Florence cathedral: Oliver Cannell

page 11: Campanile of Polish church: Maciej Laska

page 12: Church in Salzburg, Austria: Wolfgang Lienbacher

page 13: (top) Tower of Ulm Cathedral, Germany: Stefan Junger

page 13: (bottom) Double wheel window detail, Croatia: Maciej Laska

page 14: Rendering of Solomon's Temple: Matthew Alderman

page 15: Midina, Malta 'city on a hill': EPA Photo/Lino Arrigo Azzopardi

page 16: Transporting the Ark of the Covenant: Clipart.com

page 17: Tabernacle in the Wilderness: Clipart.com

page 18: Model of Jerusalem city detail: Stasys Eidiejus

page 19: Salomonic columns, cloister at St. John Lateran, Rome: Bart Parren

page 20: Midina, Malta 'city on a hill': EPA Photo/Lino Arrigo Azzopardi

page 21: Column ruins, Rome: Istockphoto, Inc.

page 22: St. Paul Outside-the-Walls, Rome: Corel

page 23: Arch of Constantine, Rome: Paolo Piccolo

page 24: (top) Ancient Roman temple ruins: Lautaro Gonda

page 24: (bottom) Pagan basilica of Maxentius: Corel

page 25: (top) Temple of Divus Romulus, Rome: Oliver Cannell

page 25: (bottom) Old St. Peter's Basilica, Rome: Clipart.com

page 26: Arch of Constantine, Rome: Paolo Piccolo

page 27: (top) St. Paul Outside-the-Walls, Rome: Corel

page 27: (bottom) Santa Sabina Church, Rome: Duncan G. Stroik

page 28: Santa Maria Maggiore, Rome: John Rattle

page 29: (top) Temple of Saturn: Oliver Cannell

page 29: (bottom) Fresco, Agia Triada, Crete, Greece: Paul Cowan

page 30: St. Basil's Cathedral, Moscow: Philip Sigin-Lavdanski

page 31: Rila monastery, Bulgaria: EPA Photo/Mladen Antonov

page 32: (top) Hagia Sophia interior detail, Constantinople: Dan Chatham

page 32: (bottom) Rendering of Hagia Sophia façade: Nicholas Daveline

page 33: (top) Rila monastery, Bulgaria: Angela Davis

page 33: (bottom): Church at Pecs, Hungary: Elvira Schaefer

page 34: (top) Palatine Chapel, Palermo, Sicily: Bart Parren

page 34: (bottom) Monastery of St. Luke of Stiris, Greece: Corel

page 35: (top) Rotunda church, Sofia, Bulgaria: EPA Photo/Vassil Donev

page 35: (bottom) Greek dome, Santorini, Greece: Angelika Stern

page 36: Upinski Cathedral, Helsinki, Finland: EPA Photo

page 37: (top) Rendering of San Marco Cathedral, Venice: Matthew Alderman

page 37: (bottom) San Marco cathedral and piazza, Venice: Serban Enache

page 38: Rendering of Mont Saint-Michel, France: Michael Ryan

page 39: St. Denis portal, France: Bart Parren

page 40: (top) Interior of Pisa Cathedral, Italy: Jean-Yves Benedeyt

page 40: (bottom) Santa Maria Torcella, Italy: Corel

page 41: (top) Pisa Cathedral. Italy: Serban Enache

page 41: (bottom) San Giovanni, Messina, Sicily: Corel

page 42: (top) Mainz Cathedral, Germany: Sue Ding

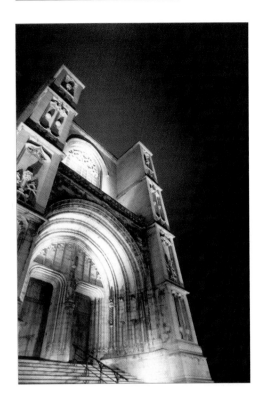

page 75: (top) St. Walburga's Church interior, Bruges, Belgium: Michael S. Rose
page 75: (bottom) Chapel at Prague Castle, Czech Republic: Celia Martinez
page 76: (top) St. Nikolas Church, Prague, Czech Republic: Corel
page 76: (bottom) Church at Plaza de Armas, Cuzco, Peru: Emmanuel Vivier
page 77: San Francisco Church, Lima, Peru: David Owens
page 78: Mariahilferkirche, Graz, Austria: Elvira Schaefer
page 79: (top) San Carlo Borromeo Church, Noto, Sicily: Fabrizio Pascucci
page 79: (bottom) Mexico City Cathedral, Mexico: Alvaro Heinzen
page 80: Baroque South American church: Corel
page 81: (top) Mission-style church: Corel
page 81: (bottom) Belltower, Santa Prisca, Taxco, Mexico: Jeffrey Logan
page 82: (top) Graz Cathedral, Austria: Graz Tourism
page 82: (bottom) St. Peter's Church interior, Munich, Germany: Corel
page 83: Church in Lima, Peru: David Owens
page 84: Sacré Coeur Basilica, Paris, France: John Rattle
page 85: Basilica of the Immaculate Conception: Washington D.C., Corel
page 86: (top) Sacred Coeur Basilica, Paris: Stella Smid-van Duijvendijk
page 86: (bottom) Brompton Oratory façade, London: Michael S. Rose
page 87: (top) Bell tower, Brazil: Micah Goulart
page 87: (bottom) Brompton Oratory sanctuary, London: Michael S. Rose
page 88: Immaculate Conception Church, Mayfair, London: Michael S. Rose
page 89: (top) St. Patrick Church, Soho Square, London: Michael S. Rose
page 89: (bottom) Westminster Cathedral, London: Michael S. Rose
page 90: Santa Maria Church, Dominican Republic: A. Fernandes
page 91: (top) St. Nicholas Church, Cali, Colombia: Michael S. Rose
page 91: (bottom) Mission-style church, Florida: Kaycee Craig
page 92: (top) La Ermita Church, Cali, Colombia: Michael S. Rose
page 92: (bottom) Mission-style church, Florida: Colleen Coombe
page 93: St. Francis Church, Santa Fe, New Mexico: Shelby Gannon
page 94: (top) St. John Cathedral, Savannah, Georgia: Greg Wolkins
page 94: (bottom) Sagrada Familia Church, Barcelona: Alexandre Savreux
page 95: Sagrada Familia tower detail, Barcelona: Chris Schmidt
page 96: St. Louis Basilica, Missouri: Karen Grotzinger
page 97: (top) St. Patrick's Cathedral, New York City: Ireneusz Skorupa
page 97: (bottom) St. Patrick's Cathedral, New York City: Ginger Garvey
page 98: Church steeple, New Zealand: Jeffrey Vella
page 99: Notre Dame du Haut, Ronchamp, France: Dan Delgado
page 100: (top) Rio de Janeiro Cathedral, Brazil: Corel
page 100: (bottom) St. Aloysius Gonzaga Church, Cincinnati: Michael S. Rose
page 101: (top) Holy Trinity Church, Vienna: Art Today
page 101: (bottom) Notre Dame du Haut, Ronchamp, France: Dan Delgado
page 102: (top) modern Belgian church: Nicole Mannens
page 102: (bottom) Stained glass, Buckfast Abbey, England: Matthew Maude
page 103: (top) St. Ignatius Chapel, Seattle, Washington: Zico Ting
page 103: (bottom) Jubilee church, Rome: Richard Meier
page 104: (top) Our Lady of the Angels Cathedral: Jordon Cooper
page 104: (bottom) Jubilee church, Rome: Richard Meier
page 105: (top) Proposed model, Oakland Cathedral: Santiago Calatrava
page 105: (bottom) Proposed model, Oakland Cathedral: Santiago Calatrava
page 106: (top) St. Mary's Basilica, Covington, Kentucky: Michael S. Rose
page 106: (bottom) St. John's Church, West Chester, Ohio: Michael S. Rose
page 107: (top) St. Ambrose Church, Rochester, N.Y.: Michael McBride
page 107: (bottom) Church of the Madeleine, Bruges, Belgium: Michael S. Rose
page 108: Thomas Aquinas College Chapel, Ojai, California: Duncan G. Stroik

page 109: All Saints Church, Walton, Kentucky: Duncan G. Stroik
page 110: (top) Rendering for proposed church, Florida: Matthew Enquist
page 110: (bottom) Rendering of proposed church, Florida: Matthew Enquist
page 111: (top) San Lorenzo Church, Cali, Colombia: Michael S. Rose
page 111: (bottom) Clear Creek Monastery, Oklahoma: Matthew Enquist
page 112: (top) Clear Creek Monastery, Oklahoma: Matthew Enquist
page 112: (bottom) All Saints Church, Walton, Kentucky: Duncan G. Stroik
page 113: (top) Rendering of proposed church, N.J.: Dino Marcantonio
page 113: (bottom) Clear Creek Monastery, Oklahoma: Matthew Enquist
page 114: Architectural detail, Venice: Roland Andrijauskas
page 116: Statue of the Sacred Heart of Jesus: Dan Brandenburg
page 117: (top) Columns, St. Peter's Basilica, Rome: Bart Parren
page 117: (bottom) Decorative apse: Christen Booth
page 118: Campanile, San Marco, Venice: Emanuele Gnani
page 119: (top) Holy water font, Brussels: Michael S. Rose
page 119: (bottom) Baptistery and cathedral, Pisa: Bart Parren
page 120: Spanish mission church, Florida: Marje Cannon
page 121: (top) Santa Croce campanile, Florence: Bart Parren
page 121: (bottom) Flying buttresses: Rene Mansi
page 122: Cloister of Santander Cathedral, Spain: Ramon Vega
page 123: (top) Dome at night, Rome: Corel
page 123: (bottom) Santa Maria Maggiore interior dome, Rome: Bart Parren
page 124: Window at mission church, San Antonio, Texas: Mario Gutierrez
page 125: (top) Cupola, St. Paul Anglican Cathedral, London: Spencer Doane
page 125: (bottom) Fleche atop St. Mary's Cathedral, Sidney: Serge Kozak
page 126: Masonry vaulting: Andrea Gingerich
page 127: (top) Gargoyles, Notre Dame Cathedral, Paris: Angie Trigg
page 127: (bottom) Chi-Rho mosaic: Steve Hong
page 128: Pilar detail, Pisa Cathedral, Italy: Bart Parren
page 129: (top) San Lorenzo Church narthex, Cali, Colombia: Michael S. Rose
page 129: (bottom) Piazza San Marco, Venice: Serban Enache
page 130: (top) Pulpit, Brussels: Michael S. Rose
page 130: (bottom) Church of All Nations, Jerusalem: Moti Meiri
page 131: (top) Church spires, Riga, Latvia: EPA Photos/Normundus Mezins
page 131: (bottom) Tympanum, Chartres Cathedral, France: Bertrand Collet
page 132: Church shadow on white wall: Aleksey Lapkovsky
page 133: Doorway, Norwich Cathedral, England: Frank Wright
page 134: Sainte Wadru Church, Mons, Belgium: Chris Chevalier
page 135: Cloisters, Norwich Cathedral, England: Frank Wright

The author would like to extend a special note of thanks to his wife Barbara, Dolores Rolfes, and Leon Suprenant for their editorial assistance, and to Matthew Enquist, Domiane Forte, Heather von Mering, Nicholas Daveline, Michael Ryan, Matthew Alderman, Dino Marcantonio and Duncan G. Stroik for their assistance in providing renderings for this volume.

**Other books on church architecture issues
by Michael S. Rose:**

The Renovation Manipulation (2000)
Ugly As Sin (2001)

www.dellachiesa.com
For more resources and literature regarding
church architecture, design, restoration,
historic preservation, and sacred art visit
Michael S. Rose's *dellachiesa.com* online.